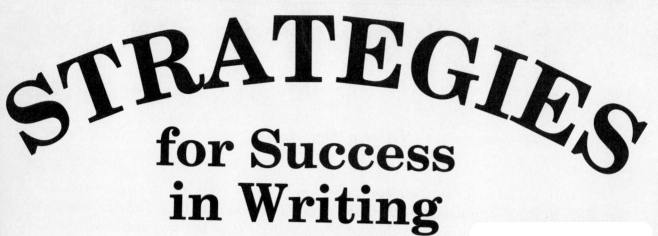

STRATEGIES
for Success in Writing

Intermediate Level

D1318727

Table of Contents

To the Student...

Our society cannot function effectively if its citizens are not capable of reading, writing, and using mathematical skills. Formal testing is the primary way we learn how well you are developing these skills. It is the way we measure both your success as a learner and our success as teachers.

The materials in this book have been given careful thought and development to assist you in learning and reinforcing the very skills you will encounter on tests. You will become aware of your strengths and weaknesses quickly through their use, so that you can practice those skills needing reinforcement.

These materials also provide you with specific test-taking strategies. You will have that extra edge you need to do well in testing situations.

You must make a commitment to yourself to do your very best to prepare for these tests. Our job is to provide you with the tools to succeed. We wish you well!

STRATEGIES
for Success in Writing

Intermediate Level

June Coultas, Ed. D. and James Swalm, Ed. D.

STECK-VAUGHN
BERRENT
PUBLICATIONS

Strategies For Success
in Writing

Intermediate Level

UNIT 1: Writing for Different Audiences

Introduction

There are many elements that go into producing a piece of good writing. Two of the critical elements are your audience and your message. In this book, we will help you develop your skills to communicate effectively what you wish to say to a specific person or group.

We will offer you opportunities to write on selected topics for different types of audiences. In addition, you will be given pieces of writing to revise and edit. These passages will help you improve your writing by giving you practice in spelling, punctuation, capitalization, and simple grammar. They will also help you when you take writing tests.

CHAPTER ONE

Audience I: Writing Letters to Family and Friends

In this chapter, we will be concentrating on writing to people we know. This usually involves the writing of letters. The topics may be quite varied, but family members or friends will be interested in reading what we have to say.

When you write to close acquaintances, you may choose to use less formal language than when you write to people you don't know. However, it is still important to pay attention to what you write and how you write it. Your first writing task will be to write a letter to a friend. The topic should be about something that happened to you in school.

A. Letter Writing

Before you write your letter, let's review the format for your letter and give you some guidance in how to organize your thoughts. Here is a sample letter format.

(Your street address)
(Your city, state, and zip code)
(Month, date, year)

(Dear _____),

    (In the **first paragraph**, tell briefly who was involved, what happened, and/or where the incident took place.)

    (In the **second paragraph**, give more information or details about the incident.)

    (In the **third or final paragraph**, summarize what happened or tell how you feel about the incident.)

(Your closing),
(Your name)

TIPS: ✓ *Remember capitals are needed in street addresses, city, state, and month.*

      ✓ *Check to see that you have included commas where they are needed. The sample letter should help you to put the commas where they belong.*

Now that we have given you a format to use, it's time to think of what you might say in your letter. We will show you what a letter to your cousin about a class trip might look like.

(Your street address)
(Your city, state, and zip code)
(Month, date, year)

(Dear _____),

Paragraph 1
Announcing the subject of the letter

    I had to write to tell you about the terrific trip our class took last week. We went to a hands-on science center. It was a long bus ride to get there, but it was worth it.

Paragraph 2
Elaboration of the trip

    You know that lots of times we go to museums and places where everybody is afraid you'll touch things or break something. Well, in this science center, you could touch everything. One exhibit showed how water could go uphill. It was called Archimedes' screw. You turned a handle in this clear plastic tube and the water traveled up the spiral axle to the top of the tube. Other exhibits showed what sound waves look like. Another one let you build an archway with blocks of wood. My favorite was trying to draw a design while looking in a mirror.

Paragraph 3
Summary

    This was a great place to visit. I was sorry when Mr. Walters told us it was time to leave. When I got home, I asked my parents if we could go back there some day when we are out of school. They promised we'd go there soon. If you and your family come for a visit this summer, maybe we could all go together. I know that you would really like it, too.

(Your closing),
(Your name)

Your Turn 1 ....

    Using these guidelines for format and organization of a letter, pick a topic and write a letter to a friend or relative. Be sure to check your letter for spelling, punctuation, and capitalization.

    On the next page are some suggested topics; however, you are free to write about something else.

Suggested Topics:

- **Your class went on an exciting trip.**

- **You turned in a report or took a test and received a very good grade.**

- **You made a team or helped your team to a winning record.**

- **You received a special prize or award.**

- **Someone came to your school and gave a special show or spoke to the students on a topic that proved to be very interesting to you.**

  or

- **Your class trip didn't turn out as you had expected.**

- **You had some problems completing a special report and got into trouble.**

- **Your team really tried hard, but didn't do too well.**

- **You are having some difficulty in school with a subject, another student, or a teacher.**

- **You think something that happened in school isn't fair.**

TIPS: ✓ *If you say you liked something **a lot**, remember **a lot** is two words.*
✓ *Also, if you sign your letter "Your friend," remember the word **friend** is spelled with an **i** before the **e**. Notice that **Your** begins with a capital letter but **friend** begins with a small letter.*

We suggest that you keep a journal for recording information that will help you reduce your writing errors. After your writing has been corrected, make a note of the types of errors you made and record them in your journal. You can put the correct spelling of words that you tend to misspell in your journal. It can become your personal dictionary to help you improve your spelling. You can do the same kind of thing for punctuation and capitalization errors, if you have difficulty remembering their correct forms.

Your Turn 2 ·····················

Write two more letters to people you know on a topic of interest to you. Here are some additional possible topics for letters. Use these topics or choose another topic from the list on the previous page.

- Thank a person for a gift that you really wanted or enjoyed receiving.
- Invite the person to visit you.
- Arrange a trip for you and your friend to take together.
- Describe a vacation you are taking or have taken recently.
- Thank a person for taking you somewhere or having you as a guest.
- Wish the person a happy holiday, a good trip, or congratulations on a special achievement.
- Inquire about what the person is doing.

You can still use the three-paragraph format for these types of letters. Of course, you may need to include more than three paragraphs in your letter. In that case, you still use the first paragraph as an introductory paragraph and the final paragraph as a summary. The paragraphs in between will be used to present different important items you wish to share with your reader.

B. Pre-Writing Content Strategy

Perhaps you found that you had difficulty writing a letter even with the strategies offered to help you with the format, the mechanics, and the suggested topics. In that case, you may need to use a pre-writing strategy to assist you in organizing what you want to say in your letter. Try this pre-writing strategy to help you overcome this problem.

Sometimes you write to a friend or relative to tell the person about a problem you have or to ask for advice. Before writing this letter, you need to consider what you want to include in it. A good way to plan what you will say is to use a mapping strategy as a pre-writing activity.

On the following page is a model of a map you might use in this situation.

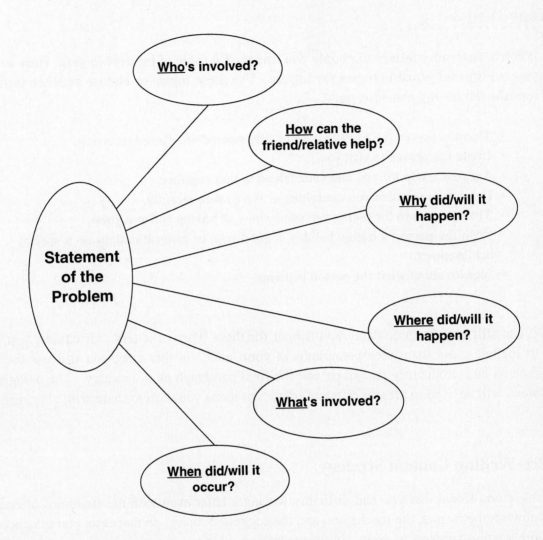

Let's use this model to map a letter to a friend in response to an invitation to a picnic.

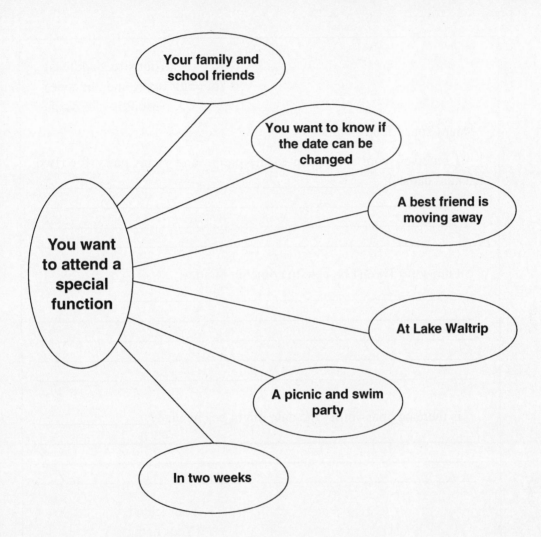

You'll notice that in constructing this particular map we asked the five "W" questions: *who, what, where, when,* and *why.* We also asked the "H" question: *how.* All maps do not require information about these six types of questions; however, it seemed appropriate in this case.

Your Turn 3 . . . .

We have written the first sentences of three paragraphs of a letter for you. Complete the paragraphs using the information contained in the sample map about the picnic and swim party.

(Your street address)
(Your city, state, and zip code)
(Month, date, year)

Dear (Your friend's name),

I received your invitation to the picnic and swim party for (two friends' names). _____

_____

_____

_____

I am sorry I won't be able to come on Sunday. _____

_____

_____

_____

_____

_____

Is there any possibility the date might be changed? _____

_____

_____

_____

Your friend,
(Your name)

Your Turn 4

For the next activity, complete your own map as a pre-writing activity and then write a letter using the ideas from your map.

Write a letter to a friend or relative telling them of a project you have to complete for a school assignment and that you need that person's help.

C. Summary

When you write to close friends and relatives, the nature of your writing is in the form of "entertainment." The content of the writing is interpersonal. The topics are closely associated with everyday activities, personal happenings, typical problems, and routine events.

The interaction between you and your audiences is generally friendly and not usually highly critical. A grandparent who receives a thank-you letter for a gift is usually delighted to hear from the grandchild. The grandparent is more interested in knowing if the child liked the gift than in being overly concerned about a minor error or two in the letter.

Friends and relatives are your most forgiving audience, as a rule. They care more about what you have to say than about how you say it. However, you should try to write clearly and correctly for any audience.

CHAPTER TWO

Audience 2: Writing for School-Related Groups

In this chapter, you will engage in writing activities for another type of audience. Rather than writing to close friends or relatives, you will be writing to a school-related audience: a teacher, a principal, a superintendent, a board of education, or a parent group. While some of the writings may take the form of letters, others will involve writing reports and short stories.

A. Writing Letters to School-Related Audiences

You will use the same format when you write letters to school-related audiences as you did when you wrote to friends or relatives. However, there will be differences in the topics, in the content, and in the organization of these letters from those you wrote to friends and relatives.

Letters to principals, superintendents, boards of education, and other school organizations have different purposes or objectives than letters written to friends or relatives. Those written to school audiences are usually written to inform the audience on a topic, to express the writer's views on a topic, to gain their support for some idea or issue, or to persuade them to change their position on some matter.

To be effective, these letters must contain carefully thought out presentations of facts to support or explain the writer's position on an issue. One way to try to ensure that these types of letters are well-organized is to use a cause and effect pre-writing map. This will help you, the writer, to organize your ideas before you compose your letter.

B. Cause and Effect Pre-Writing Strategy

Sometimes, a single cause can have several effects. At other times, each cause can have its own effect.

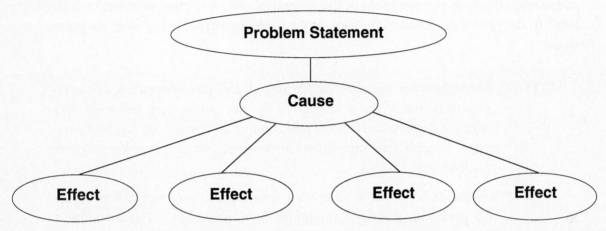

Your Turn 1
. . . .

Let's suppose that you play a musical instrument and you are interested in being in the school orchestra and/or band. However, the time for band or orchestra rehearsals has been changed. Several of the musicians are having a problem getting to the rehearsals at this new time. Write a letter to the principal explaining the problem and asking for help in solving it. Complete this map before you write your letter.

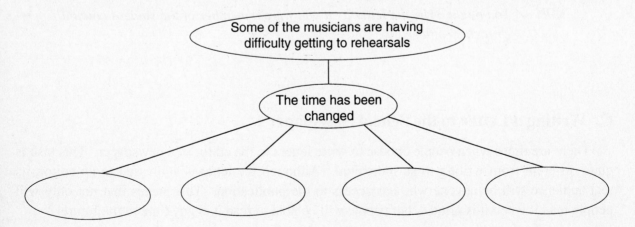

Fill in the map with the key points you wish to present to the principal to effect a change in the rehearsal time for the band or orchestra. State the problem. List the cause and effects as you see them in this situation. Provide your solution or solutions to the problem. Then write your letter to the principal using your mapping data.

> **TIP:** ✓ *We suggest you use the first paragraph to state information about the general nature of the problem. In the next paragraph, tell what difficulty the problem has caused and some of its effects. In the final paragraph, provide your suggestions on how you think the problem might be resolved.*
>
> ✓ *Remember, you want to state your concern in a way that will gain support from your principal to change the practice time. Pay attention to the tone of your letter and your choice of words. Be logical. Don't make threats or exaggerated claims about what will happen if there is no change in the situation.*

Your Turn 2

Now, write a letter to the Parent Teacher's Association thanking them for a gift they have given to your school.

Develop a cause-effect map that states the nature of the gift and how it will be beneficial to the pupils of the school. Then, write your letter to the PTA/PTO expressing your appreciation.

> **TIP:** ✓ *You might write the letter as if you were a member of the student council or a class officer.*

C. Writing a Letter to the School Newspaper

There are times when people choose to write letters to the editor of a newspaper. This task is quite different from writing to an individual. Although the letter is addressed to an editor, its real audience will be anyone who has access to the publication. This means that not only will people read it when it is printed, but people will be able to read it at any time in the future.

With this in mind, the writer should construct the letter with great care. The writer's point of view must be explained clearly with ample information to support that view. In addition, the letter should contain few, if any, errors. The audience reading this type of letter is less likely to know the writer than others to whom school-related letters are addressed. Therefore, the quality of the presentation of the letter content is very important. The writer will probably be judged on what is contained in the letter, rather than what the writer is like as an individual.

Imagine that you have been nominated by your class to run for class president. You are required to write a letter to the school newspaper outlining what you think are the important issues. The class is concerned about how you would address those concerns.

A possible pre-writing strategy would be to list the concerns of the class, as you understand them. A model for this type of pre-writing strategy might look something like this:

CONCERNS   ➞   SOLUTIONS

CONCERNS	SOLUTIONS
_____	_____
_____	_____
_____	_____
_____	_____

TIP: ✓ *In writing your letter, you will need an introductory paragraph stating that you are running for office and that you are aware of the problems that concern students.*

Each of the concerns and your solution(s) will then become paragraphs in your letter. You will need to state the problem and what you propose doing about it.

The final paragraph should summarize why you feel you are the best person for the office because of your ability to understand and solve the problems of the students in your class.

Your Turn 3

Now, make your own outline for your letter. Then, write your letter to the school newspaper.

D. Writing a Letter to the School Board

For this activity, you will be writing a letter to the president of the school board. The board has decided to have a library-media specialist in your school for only two days per week. This means that the library will either be closed for the other three days or a volunteer will be in the library on those three days.

Write a letter expressing your views on this situation. You will need to consider a pre-writing strategy that will allow you to think of the cause and effect relations you see resulting from this decision. You will need to think of whether you favor or oppose this decision and what you want the board to do about it, if anything.

The pre-writing strategy may be merely a listing of the causes on one side of a sheet of paper and the effects on the other side. Your letter would then elaborate on each of these cause and effect situations and conclude with your recommendation of what you think about the situation.

CAUSE   ⟶   EFFECT

1. _____   _____
2. _____   _____
3. _____   _____
4. _____   _____
5. _____   _____

Your Turn 4
• •

Write a letter expressing your views on the situation above. Use the Cause and Effect pre-writing strategy or another strategy that you prefer.

E. Report Writing

Students are required to write different types of reports in different academic subjects. One common report in English classes is the book report. However, science and social studies teachers frequently ask their students to write some type of report for their classes, too.

While the content and format may be different for these and other types of reports, some things are common among all of them. The writer must pay attention to the content of the report. Their teachers will look for facts and support of positions, rather than merely opinions. The mechanics of the reports will play a part in the grade assigned to these reports. We will suggest some approaches to completing some of these types of assignments.

F. Book Reports

Your English teacher has assigned a book report for the class to write. You have read an exciting novel about a professor and his family who took a summer vacation to explore for a hidden Inca treasure. To help you write your report, we suggest you use a mapping strategy to note important information to be included in your writing. Here are two sample maps.

MAP 1

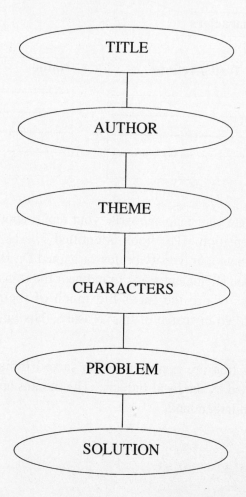

MAP 2

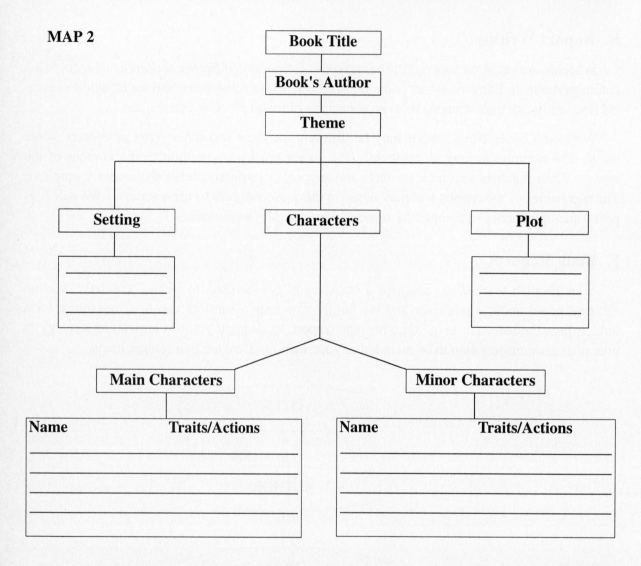

To help you complete your map and write your report about an imaginary book, we will give you some useful information. The book is entitled *The Gold Trail*, and it was written by I. Wright. The story is about a university professor named Dr. Bernardi who has spent years trying to decipher the words on an ancient stone found near the ruins of a pyramid in Central America. He believes he knows where the Incas hid much of their gold to keep it away from the Spaniards. He plans to go in search of this treasure. His family decides to accompany him on his adventure.

Unfortunately, the treasure seems to lie on sacred Indian land and the professor and his family are not welcomed by the local Indians. The Indians are suspicious of the newcomers and what they are doing on Indian land.

Before the professor can convince the Indians that they mean no harm, a heavy rainstorm in the mountains creates a flash flood and huge boulders crash into the professor's camp, injuring one of his sons badly. The family struggles to get the boy to medical help, but their camper is damaged in the rock slide.

An Indian boy tending his horses comes upon the campers and offers to get help from the Indian tribal doctor. The professor's son is treated and the family eventually is able to get help to repair their camper.

The professor does not find the hidden treasure, but he becomes friendly with the Indians and asks if he might return in the fall to learn more of their history and culture.

Your Turn 5 ....

In preparation for writing your book report, use a mapping strategy to organize the details from the imaginary book *The Gold Trail*. Choose Map 1 or Map 2. Put key facts on your map. They may include information from our story outline, or they may be things that your imagination adds to this story.

Then write your book report. Be sure to include your evaluation of the book. You can give the characters names, decide details about the setting, tell some of the action, and note the plot and the events.

Your Turn 6 ....

Using a book or a story that you have read recently, prepare a map of key elements and write a book report. You may use one of the suggested map designs or one of your own choosing in preparation for writing your report.

G. Writing a Social Studies Report

Here is another writing assignment that you might be asked to do. Your social studies teacher has asked the class to choose two important figures in history and write a report that compares and contrasts the two individuals in the following ways: their family or early life with their later rise to prominence, or their importance to their country at the time they lived with their influence on later history.

To map this type of assignment, a Venn diagram might be used. This is a type of picture that shows two overlapping circles. The outer part of the circles would indicate how the two persons were different in the key areas, and the inner circle would indicate ways in which they were alike.

The paper or report could be written with one paragraph telling similarities between the individuals, and one or more paragraphs detailing how they differed in specific ways.

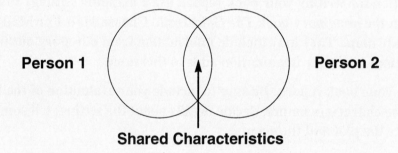

Person 1   **Person 2**

Shared Characteristics

Another strategy would be to make a comparison chart. It would include three lists.

Person #1 (Name)	Both	Person #2 (Name)

Under the "Person #1" column would be the unique characteristics of one important historical figure. Under the "Person #2" column would be the unique characteristics of the second important historical figure. Under the "Both" column would be the characteristics the two figures share in common.

> **TIP:** ✓ *This same strategy can be used whenever you are comparing likenesses or differences between two things. It can be used when you are asked to compare or contrast two things, too.*

Your Turn 7 ·······

Write a report comparing two things. Develop a Venn diagram or a comparison chart before you begin to write. Some ideas you may want to use for your assignment might include:

- Compare and contrast early explorers with the astronauts of today.

- Compare and contrast two music or movie stars that you like.

- Compare and contrast the American Revolution to the present break-up of the Soviet Union.

- Compare and contrast your math teacher and your English teacher.

H. Writing a Science Experiment

In your science class, you have just completed a very interesting experiment. Your teacher has instructed the class to explain what was done step-by-step in the experiment and to summarize the results.

To prepare for this type of writing assignment, you will need to think of the sequence of events that occurred during the experiment. Perhaps the best way to do this is to make a list and indicate what you used or did.

EXPERIMENT

Hypothesis _____

_____

Materials (if any): _____

Equipment (if any): _____

Step 1: _____

_____

Step 2: _____

_____

Step 3: _____

_____

Conclusion _____

_____

When you write your report of the experiment, you might choose to use words other than "Step 1," etc. You could use "first," "next," "following that," and "finally." Your report will need to be structured in a way that meets your teacher's guidelines for science reports. Check with your teacher before you write your assignment. If no format is preferred, you are free to write your report in the manner that suits you best.

Here is an example of the model for a science experiment.

Imagine that a science experiment involves getting a shelled hard-boiled egg into a narrow-necked glass bottle and out again intact. The experiment is a demonstration of how air pressure works and how heated air molecules result in less air pressure.

Hypothesis: The egg will fit into the bottle because of the heat.

Materials (if any): 1 hard-boiled shelled egg

Equipment (if any): The equipment includes a glass bottle with a neck opening too small for the egg to slip though, a shelled hard-boiled egg, a long match, and a long strip of folded paper.

Step 1: The paper is placed into the glass bottle.

Step 2: The long match is lit and placed into the bottle, lighting the paper.

Step 3: The shelled hard-boiled egg is placed into the open-necked bottle.

Step 4: The egg is gradually drawn into the bottle.

Step 5: The egg falls to the bottom of the bottle.

Step 6: Air is blown or forced into the up-turned bottle.

Step 7: The egg comes back out of the bottle intact.

Conclusion: The heated air caused the air molecules to expand and reduce the air pressure inside the bottle. The outer air pressure was greater and the egg was pushed inside the bottle.

When air was blown into the bottle, the air pressure inside the bottle was greater than the air pressure outside the bottle, and the egg was forced back out of the bottle.

This experiment helps to demonstrate that hot air is lighter and rises while cool air is heavier and falls.

Your Turn 8 . . . .

Write a report for an imaginary science experiment that you would like to conduct, or for an experiment that you actually conducted in your science class.

I. Story Writing

Another common assignment is to write a story. This narrative form of writing is part of most English classes. Sometimes, the writers are given writing prompts to suggest the general content of a story. At other times, they are given only general suggestions as to what topics they might write about, or they might be free to choose their own topics.

Whatever the specific task, there are some commonalities that writers need to consider in developing their stories. All stories have a plot, a character or characters, and a setting. In a pre-writing mapping exercise, the writer might include all or only one of these key elements in a map. The choice will probably depend upon what is the most important part of the story the writer has in mind.

If the story is to focus primarily on a character or several characters, then the map may be used to explore the various aspects of the characters, e.g., size, age, personality, role in the story. In the event that the plot is the most important part of the story, then the map could focus on the events that the writer intends to use in the development of the plot.

PLOT OUTLINE

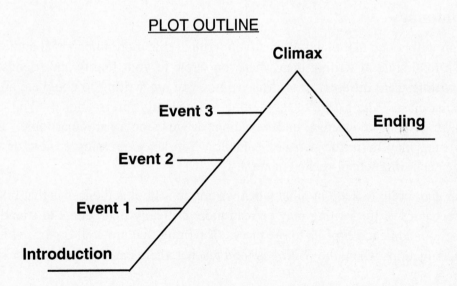

The beginning of a story must capture the readers' interest so they will read the rest of the story. Then, the events in the plot draw the readers along until the climax of the story is reached. This may be the end of the story. However, the writer may continue with some other appropriate ending that might provide an answer to a situation, offer an explanation or solution to a problem, or provide some twist to the story or surprise ending. Sometimes, readers are left to draw their own conclusions about what happened, why it happened, who was involved, who committed the act, or what might happen in the future.

In other words, it isn't necessary for the writer to answer all of the questions posed in the plot. All stories do not have "happy endings." Readers can be left wondering how things will turn out.

TIP: ✓ *After you have written an interesting and perhaps suspenseful story or adventure, don't spoil the effect by having the main character wake up, revealing that the story is only a dream. The story will be more impressive if the readers are left to wonder if the tale is real or a dream.*

Your Turn 9 ....
• • • • • • • • • • • • • • • • • •

Imagine that you are a visitor at the White House in Washington, D.C., and you are mistaken for someone else. Because of this mistaken identity, you are invited to spend the weekend at the White House. Write a story about that weekend. Remember to make a plot outline first, then write your story.

J. Summary

You will notice that much of what you write to this more impersonal audience will involve a more formal style of writing than when you wrote to your family and friends. The subjects of your writing were different, too. Many times you are writing to complete an assignment for a particular class. The nature of the writing is frequently informational. You are being asked to demonstrate your knowledge, understanding, or views on a particular topic. In some instances, the writing may be in the persuasive mode. You are expressing a view or wish to see some change occur in a school-related matter.

Another point to keep in mind when writing to school audiences is that both the content and the mechanics of the writing may be read more critically than letters to friends tend to be read. This school audience expects to see pieces of writing that are well-organized and correctly written. In situations where the writing is for a teacher, there can be a penalty for submitting poorly-written work.

Even in those cases when you are writing to the principal, the board of education, or some school group, there is a kind of penalty that may arise from a carelessly prepared letter. You may not have presented your position so that the person or group receiving the letter understands. Moreover, a letter filled with mechanical errors may create a negative impression on the readers, and you will not achieve your desired results.

What should you do when you are writing to this type of audience?

- **Spend time in the pre-writing stage planning what you want to say.**
- **Write a first draft and then revise the organization and content of what you have written.**
- **Read the revised piece and edit it for spelling, capitalization, punctuation, and grammatical errors.**
- **Rewrite the revised draft, if needed.**

A major mistake that writers make is submitting a paper that is really only a first draft, rather than a final draft that has been revised and edited. Often, students don't want to take the time to write a paper more than once. However, the added time to produce a better piece of writing will probably have a significant impact upon the results it achieves.

CHAPTER THREE

Audience 3: Writing Letters to People You Don't Know

In this chapter, you will have opportunities to practice writing to a third type of audience. This audience is one that is less well-known to you personally and may represent a group of people rather than a single individual.

Your audience might be the advice columnist in a local newspaper, the board of education, the mayor of your town or another government official, the editor of a newspaper, or some business or organization. In most cases, you will be writing about some issue or problem that is of concern to you, and you want to share your views on it.

This is a more difficult type of writing than writing to a good friend. You have to pay attention to the tone of your letter, the way you organize your content, and the mechanics. You want to make a very good impression on your audience so they will carefully read and consider what you have to say.

Let's look at some of the types of writing we might do for this kind of audience. We'll begin with the business letter.

A. Business Letters

When we become adults, we write many more business letters than we do friendly letters. We write these letters for many different reasons.

On the next page is a mapping exercise for you to complete. Try to identify as many reasons as you can why people might need to write business letters. You may need to add additional circles to this model.

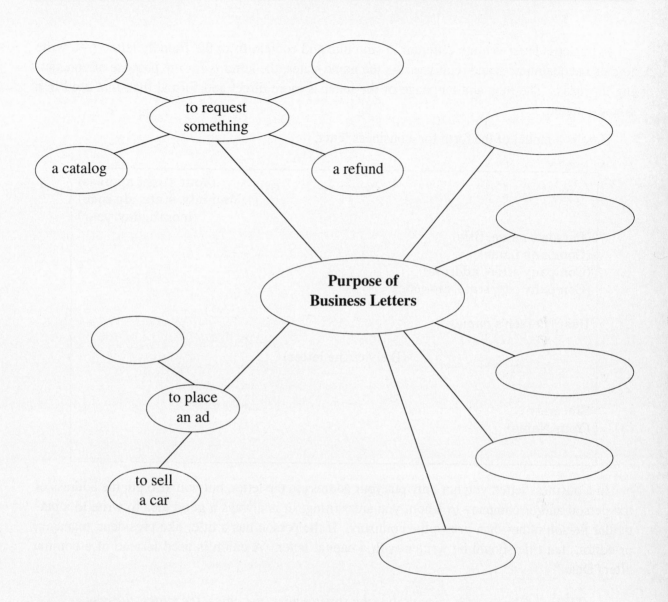

Your Turn 1

Select a purpose for writing a business letter. Prepare a map of what you need to include in your letter. Then, write the letter. You can use an imaginary person, company, address, etc.

A business letter is quite different in structure and content from the friendly letters you write to close acquaintances and relatives. As the name states, the letter is for the purpose of conducting business. The tone and language of the letter is more direct and formal than that used in a friendly letter.

Here is a model of the form for a business letter.

```
                                                    (Your street address)
                                                    (Your city, state, zip code)
                                                    (month, day, year)

(Person's name, title)
(Company name)
(Company street address)
(Company city, state, zip code)

Dear (Person's name):

                    (Body of the letter)



Sincerely,
(Your Name)
```

In a business letter, you not only put your address in the letter, but you also put the address of the person and/or company to whom you are writing. It is always a good idea to write to a particular person rather than just to the company. If the person has a title, like president, manager, or editor, that title should be written with a capital letter. A colon is used instead of a comma after "Dear."

> **TIPS:** ✓ *Remember to capitalize the street names, the cities, the states, the company name, and the month. The closing is also capitalized, unless you use more than one word. Then, only the first word is capitalized, e.g.,* **Yours truly** *or* **Very truly yours**. *Note that* **truly** *does not have an* **e** *in it.*

You can use the three-paragraph model for your business letter. The first paragraph briefly states the reason why you are writing the letter. The second paragraph explains in more detail what you want the person to know about the situation. The final paragraph tells what you hope will happen or what you want the person to do about the situation.

Your Turn 2

• • • • • • • • • • • • • • • • • •

Using the three-paragraph model, write a business letter using the format from the previous page. Be sure to capitalize proper nouns.

B. Persuasive Letter

Another type of letter that you might write could be one in which you are trying to inform someone about a situation and persuade that person to take some desired action. This letter follows the form of the business letter. However, it is often written using more emotional language than we use in typical business letters.

The persons to whom we direct these persuasive letters are frequently governmental persons. They are people with the power to effect change. When people don't like something that is happening in the country, they may write to their senators or representatives in Washington. When they don't approve of some local matters, they may write to the mayor and council. In other words, they write to the person who they feel can best respond to their concerns.

It is important to remember that not all letters complain about something. Frequently, people write letters thanking someone for something that was done for them or that they liked.

The next few activities will give you opportunities to write letters to different members of this broader and more distant audience on some specific topics.

Let's suppose you are concerned about how dangerous it is for people to cross a street or streets in your neighborhood where there are no traffic lights. If you want something done to correct this situation, you will probably need to write to some government officials in your town or to the local newspaper. These people will probably be strangers to you. So, you will need to plan carefully and in some detail what you want to say, if you hope to have them do something to resolve the problem.

To get action on this problem, you might write to one or more of the following:

- **the mayor and council**

- **the chief of police or the department of public safety**

- **your state senator or representative**

- **the editor of your local newspaper**

Before you write your letter, it is important to engage in a pre-writing activity to help you organize the ideas to be included in your letter. Here is one way you might go about mapping this letter.

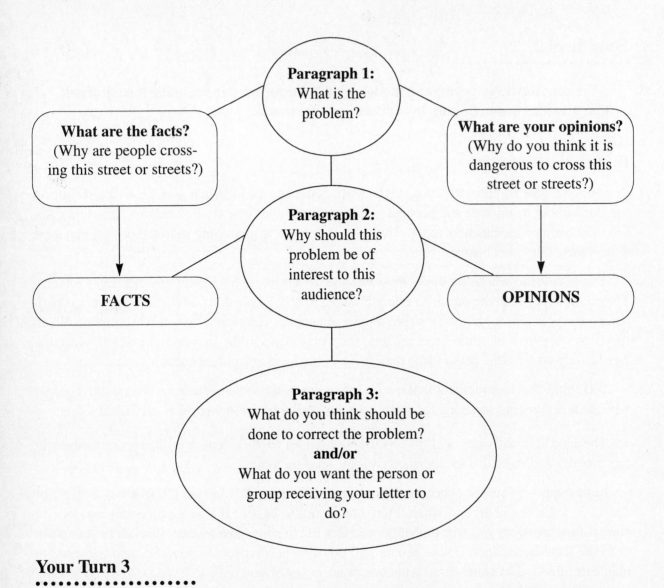

Your Turn 3

Using this pre-writing model, fill in the information that you might include in your letter about the danger of crossing a busy street in your neighborhood.

Then, write a letter to a person or group who you think can help resolve this problem. Be sure to state your problem in the first paragraph of your letter. In the second paragraph, you can go into greater detail about your concerns or cite some situations that support your position. In the final paragraph, you may offer your suggestion(s) about what you think should be done, or you might ask the person to investigate the situation.

TIP: ✓ *Be sure to check your letter for spelling, punctuation, and*
capitalizations.

C. Letters to Advice Columnists

There are times when people feel they need to share their problems with someone. Frequently, they choose to write to an advice columnist. They may have tried on their own to resolve their problems, but they may be dissatisfied with the result or wish to know if they took the appropriate action.

In the pre-writing map below, we have sketched the basic structure of a letter to an advice columnist. On the left hand side are the specifics of the problem, while on the right side are the two vital components of any such letter.

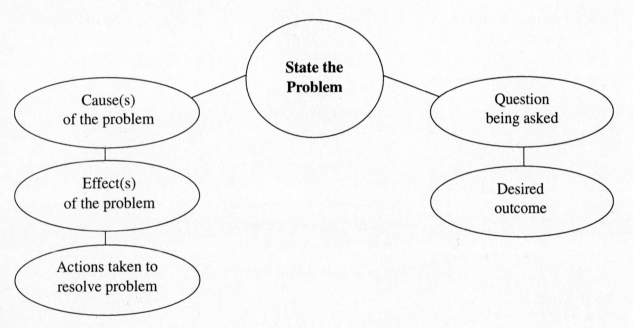

Your Turn 4

Think of some problem that you might want to ask an advice columnist either to get help on how to resolve a problem or to find out if what you have been doing to resolve the problem is appropriate.

Map the information about your problem.

Let's try another example. You are concerned because your friends are teasing you. It bothers you. You have decided to write a letter to an advice columnist in the local paper. You hope this person can offer a suggestion on how you can solve your problem.

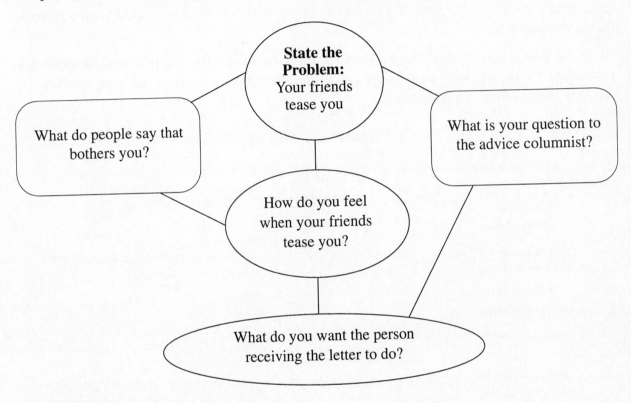

Your Turn 5
• • • • • • • • • • • • • • • • • •

Let's assume that you have moved and are attending a new school. You have always been able to make friends easily. In your other school, you had lots of friends and were involved in many activities. You have had difficulty adjusting to your new school and making friends.

Develop a map containing information about this situation. Then, use the letter format on the next page to write to an advice columnist.

In paragraph 1, describe your problem and some of the background information important to understanding it.

In paragraph 2, describe your expectations about coming to a new school, and your concerns since you have arrived there.

In paragraph 3, tell what you have done since entering the new school to resolve your problem, and ask for advice to solve your problem.

After completing the pre-writing map strategy, write your letter to the advice columnist. Use this model for your letter.

	Dear Alexandra:
Paragraph 1:	I am a new student in the middle school.
	_____
Paragraph 2:	I thought it would be fun coming to a new town and meeting new people.
	_____
Paragraph 3:	I've tried several ways to let the kids know that I want to be friends.
	_____

For this next activity, imagine that the problem you shared with the advice columnist was that you have grown very tall this year. You are taller than all of your friends. They are teasing you and maybe calling you names because you're so tall.

Your Turn 6
• • • • • • • • • • • • • • • • • • •

Design a map expressing the problem, the things that your friends are saying, and how these things are affecting you. Be sure to include the question you want the advice counselor to answer. After you complete the map, write your letter to the columnist.

D. Writing Letters to a Newspaper

There are other people and groups to whom you might write letters, including the editor of a local newspaper. You will need to think of how to present your ideas with supporting data to make others pay attention to what you have to say. As indicated in the pre-writing map below, a letter to a newspaper would typically include the writer's opinions as well as facts and details that support these opinions. Much of the information you learned in Chapter 2 relating to writing to a school newspaper would apply here.

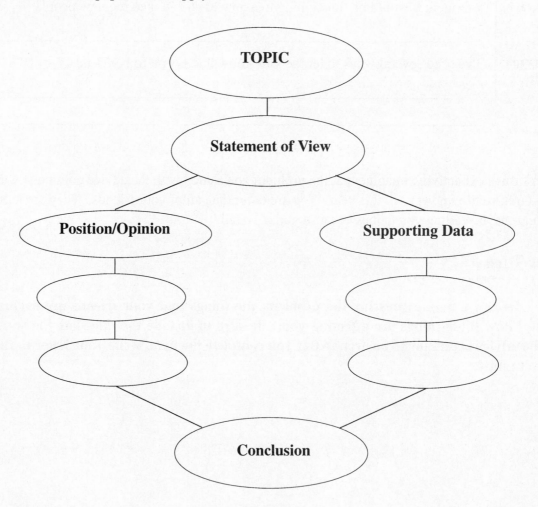

Your Turn 7

Design a map and write a letter to the theater manager or to the editor of the local newspaper expressing your views on the increase in the cost of attending a movie.

E. Summary

This third type of audience is composed of persons or groups with whom the writer has the least direct connections. This means that whatever is written to them must be very well-expressed and correct. The audience has no reason to pay more attention to your letter than to anyone else's. It's not like writing to a favorite relative or even to your science teacher.

Think of yourself as a salesperson. You must create a piece of highly persuasive writing if you are to achieve any desired result. For example, why do you want to buy a specific brand of sneakers or jeans? It is because you have been persuaded that there is something about them that makes you want to own them. Often, they are more expensive than other brands, but that doesn't make a difference to you. You have been persuaded to purchase them. This is similar to letters you write to get people to do what you want them to do. You need to express your position in such a compelling way that the person or group will be persuaded to respond to you in the way you wish.

As a result of the work you have done in these first three chapters, you are now familiar with the characteristics of three audiences for whom you may be expected to write. Now, we will concentrate on some specific revising and editing situations to help you produce a better final draft of your writing.

UNIT 2: Revising Written Work

Introduction

This unit is devoted to the part of the writing process that is known as revision. Once the first draft of a piece of writing has been completed, the writer must go back and read what has been written. No serious writer expects to produce a perfect piece of writing the first time. There are ways that the content can be reorganized to improve the writing.

In revising the text, the writer looks for ways that the information may be changed to improve the flow of the story, the report, the letter, or other piece of writing. By moving a sentence or a paragraph in the text, the writer can often improve the quality of the writing and help the reader to better understand the meaning.

Sometimes, the writer may put some unnecessary information in the writing. This irrelevant material can be distracting to the reader's comprehension of the text. It can detract from the quality of the writing. These sentences should be eliminated from the final draft of the piece.

A third problem that requires revision is a poor transition from one paragraph or thought to the next. This may involve the use of a single transitional word or it may require the use of a complete sentence. In any case, the writer is trying to help the reader to follow the line of the text in the most logical way. This will help the reader to comprehend the message the writer is trying to present.

Another type of revision involves rewriting sentences that contain flaws in their structure. These problems may relate to correct verb form or subject and verb agreement. It may be that phrases are not written in parallel form. Sometimes pronouns are the incorrect form, or they are used in a way that makes it difficult to know to what nouns they refer.

Finally, revision may include combining several sentences to form one sentence. It may also involve changing the order of phrases or clauses to make the sentences more interesting to read.

CHAPTER FOUR

Revising Text

A. Content Organization

In this chapter, you will have the opportunity to make revisions to texts to improve the reader's ability to understand the message the writer wishes to convey. You will be able to select good transitional words to begin new paragraphs. In addition, you will be able to suggest where some sentences or paragraphs might be placed in the text to help readers understand the meaning of the text. You will also be able to identify sentences that are irrelevant to the content and that should be omitted from the text.

You will be given examples of each of these three types of revisions. Then, you will be given some pieces of text and asked to identify what revisions, if any, are needed to aid the reader in comprehending the writer's intended message. Explanations of why certain answers are correct while others are incorrect follow each section.

In the sample letter below we have included examples of the three types of revisions. There is a sentence that should be moved to a new location, a sentence that is irrelevant to the content of the letter, and the need for a transitional word between two paragraphs. We will ask multiple-choice questions at the end of the letter about how you would go about improving the content through these revisions.

✏ Shanna Writes to Her Grandmother

1   Dear Grammy,

2   I want to invite you to come to Grandparents' Day at
3   my school. It is on May 2. The program starts at 9:00 A.M.
4   in my classroom.

5   In social studies, we are studying about Latin American
6   countries. I told my teacher and my class about your trips
7   to some of these countries. They want you to bring your
8   videos or slides of the countries you have visited. I know
9   they will be especially interested in the people and in the
10   history of these countries. The schedule includes participating
11   in all of my morning classes and helping me with my class
12   assignments.

13   After social studies, we will spend time reading our new

14   novel about Latin America and writing about what we have learned

15   from this book about the people. You can help me with my

16   composition. Usually, I don't receive a very good grade on my

17   compositions. I'm doing much better in my math now.

18   The class has written a play entitled "Grandparents, Our

19   Special Friends." I still need a lot of practice in my writing.

20   I was one of the major writers of the play. It says how I really

21   feel about you. I think you will like it.

22   For lunch, you can either eat with me in our cafeteria or

23   take me out for lunch. The cafeteria food is okay, but you

24   might like McDonald's better. I'll leave that up to you.

25   If we eat in the cafeteria, you may meet some of my friends

26   who eat at my table. I don't think they will all go out for

27   lunch.

28   I hope you can come. We can have a lot of fun together.

29   Your loving granddaughter,

         Shanna

1. Where should the sentence in lines 10-12 be moved to improve the organization of the text ("The...assignments.")?

     A. after lines 2-3 ("I...school.")
     B. after lines 3-4 ("The...classroom.")
     C. after lines 16-17 ("Usually...compositions.")
     D. after line 21 ("I...it.")

2. Which sentence can be deleted because it is not a relevant detail?

     A. lines 3-4 ("The...classroom.")
     B. lines 7-8 ("They...visited.")
     C. line 17 ("I'm...now.")
     D. lines 26-27 ("I...lunch.")

3. Which would be the best transition word to use before the sentence in line 19 ("I...play.")?

     A. Therefore,
     B. Moreover,
     C. Although,
     D. However,

See page 43 for answers and explanations for the three questions.

In this activity, we have given you help in revising the letter by identifying what revisions are needed. However, when you are doing your own writing, you will need to look for these types of revisions on your own.

Your Turn 1

Your social studies teacher has asked your class to write what changes might occur if a woman were elected president of the country. Kurt wrote this report:

✏ If a Woman Became President

1   There would be some changes in our country if a woman became
2   president. I think there would be more peace. But, I don't think there
3   would be as many things different as some people say.

4   A woman president might be more interested in children's safety,
5   in education, and in health care. Men say they care about these
6   things, but they don't seem to pass laws that really help children and
7   families.

8   If a woman were president, I think we wouldn't get into wars and
9   send planes to bomb people. My mother gets angry when she sees
10 these things on TV. Men seem to be more ready to fight than women.
11 A woman might put the money used for wars into other programs.

12 It wouldn't be easy to be the first woman to be president. People
13 would be watching everything she did and saying that a man
14 wouldn't do that or a man would do it better.

In this piece of writing, make the following revisions:

1. **Which sentence should be moved to a different place in the text? Copy the sentence and tell where you think it fits better.**

2. **What would be a good transitional word to use in the second paragraph?**

3. **Is there a sentence that should be deleted because it doesn't support the main theme of the text? If you were going to delete a sentence, which one would it be?**

4. **Are there any other revisions you would make? If so, what are they?**

See page 44 for answers and explanations for the report.

Your Turn 2

Darshan wrote a letter to the editor of the local newspaper. He was concerned about what someone had written about students entering the school from other countries.

After reading the first draft of his letter, make the appropriate revisions.

✏ Letter to the Editor

1   To the Editor:

2   I am very concerned about a recent letter that appeared in your
3 letter to the editor column. It was about people coming to the United
4 States. The letter writer said, "These people don't want to learn
5 English. They want to be taught in their own language. Why should
6 we have special programs to teach them English?"

7   Many people coming to the United States don't know English. They
8 really do want to learn to speak the language. Some have studied it
9 in their schools, but it is different when they come to this country.
10 People speak faster, and it is hard to follow what they are saying.
11 Also, the accent is different.

12   It isn't easy to learn a new language. It takes time. He said that
13 these people are lazy.

14   How would you feel if you were in a school and everyone was talk-
15 ing a language that you didn't understand? You are trying to learn,
16 but it is very difficult. Do you speak another language?

See page 45 for answers and explanations for Your Turn 2.

Selection #2

In this activity, Terry is writing a letter to the school principal. Terry is concerned about a final exam. As you read her letter, look for possible errors.

✏ Letter to the Principal

1   Dear Mrs. Castellano,

2   I am writing to you to complain about something that happen
3   last week. As you know, we began taking our final exams then.
4   Our English exam was on Wednesday.

5   We start review for the exam the week before. Mr. Hamilton
6   told us that we would have to define 25 words. We would have
7   to write a sentence for each. We would have questions
8   about the novels we read this year. We would be asked things
9   like character and plot. There would be an essay to write,
10   too.

11   That was okay. But, when we got the exam things weren't
12   what we studied. There were eight words that we never had.
13   Even the questions about the novels were different. We were
14   asked to compare the themes of two novels. And to describe
15   how the main characters in those novels would act in three
16   different situations.

17   Some of us complained to Mr. Hamilton that we never studied
18   some of the words in class. He just said that lots of times we'll be
19   tested on new words. We don't like to take tests, usually.

20   We told him that we didn't understand what he was asking on
21   some of the questions about the novels. They weren't things we had
22   spent time discussing in class. He said we must not have been paying
23   attention in class.

24   I've talked to many of the other kids. They all feel like I do. The
25   test wasn't fare. We really did study what we were told would be on
26   the test.

27   Probably, we'll pass, but a poor final test grade could keep some of
28   us off the honor roll. It just doesn't seem right.

29   We think you should do something about this.

Terry

Your task is to revise this letter to the principal.

1. What change is needed in the first sentence ("I...week.")?

   The answer is _____.

   HINT: *Think about verb tense.*

2. What change could be made in line 5 in paragraph 2?

   The answer is _____.

   HINT: *Think about the verb tense.*

3. How could you revise the sentences in lines 5-9 ("Mr....plot.")?

   The answer is _____.

   HINT: *a. Make two sentences.*
   b. Make a compound sentence.
   c. Use a colon and make a list.

   Try to revise this section in more than one way.

4. Try to improve the opening sentence in paragraph 3.

   HINT: *You might substitute one word for another in the sentence.*

5. How can you combine the sentences in lines 13-16 ("Even...situations.")?

   The answer is _____.

   HINT: *Is **and** a good word to use to begin a sentence?*

   What else could you do to improve one or both of these sentences?

6. What should be corrected in lines 24-25 ("The...fare.")?

   The answer is _____.

7. What sentence should be eliminated in the letter?

   The answer is _____.

8. What would be a good transitional word to use at the beginning of paragraph 4?

   The answer is _____.

Your Turn 3
• • • • • • • • • • • • • • • • • • •

At one time or another, everyone thinks something is unfair. Sometimes a person is right and sometimes not. People look at things differently. What seems fair to one person may seem unfair to another.

A. Write a letter from the principal to Terry, explaining what action, if any, will be taken in this matter.

B. Write about something that you think is unfair. Suggest what you think should be done to correct the problem.

TIP: ✓ Use a pre-writing strategy to help you organize your thoughts on the topics. Be sure to reread your letters to try to find and correct errors.

Selection #3

In this activity, Reggie is writing to a U.S. Senator about a problem.

✏ Dear Senator

1   Dear Senator Langston:

2   I think their is a serious problem that needs your help. People in
3   our town are trying to help the homeless.

4   Our schools collect food. Our schools collect clothing for needy
5   families. Our churches have food pantries. Our churches have soup
6   kitchens to feed the hungry people. At least four times every year,
7   my parents work with others at a nearby church to set up beds and
8   make meals for people who are looking for places to live.

9   Lots of people don't know that so many homeless people are just
10   little kids. They can't help it if their parents aren't together. Their
11   apartments burned down. Their parents work, but can't find an
12   apartment they can afford.

13   I keep hearing on TV that lots of people are out of work or are
14   losing their jobs. I wonder. Can't some of these people help build
15   houses for the homeless? It think that could help solve the problem of
16   homelessness. Many people own their own homes.

17   I know you have lots of things to worry about; but, I think you
18   should work on this problem. Little kids should have a home. They
19   can't do much about it. But, you're an adult, and I think your job is to
20   help people. My father says that's what senators are elected to do.

                  Your friend,

21   *Reggie*

Using this letter, answer the following revision questions.

1. What correction is needed in line 2? Why?

   _____

2. What is the best way to combine the sentences in lines 4-6 ("Our...people.")?

   _____

3. How can you combine the sentences in lines 10-12 ("They...afford.")?

   _____

4. What would be a good word to join the sentences in lines 18-19 ("Little...it.")?

   _____

5. What sentence should be deleted?

   _____

Your Turn 4
• • • • • • • • • • • • • • • • • • •

Write a letter to some important person telling that person about some problem you think that person should help to solve. After you write your first draft, go back and revise your letter. Remember, a person will be more favorably impressed by a letter that is well-written than by one that contains errors.

One of the most difficult parts of revision involves combining sentences to make more interesting sentences. Some of these revisions are needed when there are incomplete sentences or run-on sentences in the text that must be corrected. The following story is a first draft that was written as an English assignment. You are to read the story and answer the questions about ways to revise some of the sentences in the the text.

Selection #4

✏ A Game of Stickball

1	Jarrod and Leon were playing in a vacant lot. Not too far from
2	their apartment house. Leon was hitting rocks with a stick. One of the
3	rocks sailed higher and farther. Than he had ever hit a rock before.
4	Jarrod stared in disbelief at Leon's amazing hit it went clear out of the
5	lot.
6	The boys heard a noise. Jarrod was sure it was the sound of glass
7	breaking. He turned and looked at Leon. Jarrod was afraid to say
8	what he was thinking.
9	Leon heard the same sound. He didn't want to think that his fan-
10	tastic hit was anything but a homer with bases loaded that cleared
11	the center field wall. However, he wasn't sure. That noise sure did
12	sound like breaking glass.
13	The boys looked at each other for a few seconds. Leon shrugged
14	his shoulders and headed in the direction of the noise. Jarrod wasn't
15	sure he wanted to know what made the noise but he couldn't let Leon
16	down. They were best friends besides maybe the next time it would
17	be his turn to hit the homer.

1. What is the best way to correct the sentences in lines 1-2 ("Jarrod...house.")?

   A. Jarrod and Leon were playing. In a vacant lot. Not too far from their apartment house.

   B. Jarrod and Leon were playing. In a vacant lot not too far from their apartment house.

   C. Jarrod and Leon were playing in a vacant lot not too far from their apartment house.

   D. Make no change.

2. What is the best way to correct the sentences in lines 2-3 ("One...before.")?

   A. One of the rocks sailed higher and farther than he had ever hit a rock before.

   B. One of the rocks. Sailed higher and farther than he had ever hit a rock before.

   C. One of the rocks sailed. Higher and farther than he had every hit a rock before.

   D. One of the rocks sailed. Higher and farther. Than he had ever hit a rock before.

3. What change, if any, is needed to correct this sentences in lines 4-5 ("Jarrod...lot.")?

   A. Jarrod stared in disbelief. At Leon's amazing hit. It went clear out of the lot.

   B. Jarrod stared in disbelief at Leon's amazing hit. It went clear out of the lot.

   C. Jarrod stared in disbelief. Leon's amazing hit it went clear out of the lot.

   D. Jarrod stared in disbelief at Leon's amazing hit, it went clear out of the lot.

4. What change, if any, is needed in the sentences in lines 9-11 ("He...wall.")?

   A. He didn't want to think that his fantastic hit was anything but a homer. With bases loaded that cleared the center field wall.

   B. He didn't want to think that his fantastic hit was anything but a homer with bases loaded. That cleared the center field wall.

   C. He didn't want to think. His fantastic hit was a homer with bases loaded that cleared the center field wall.

   D. Make no change.

5. What change, if any, is needed in the sentences in lines 14-16 ("Jarrod...down.")?

  A. Jarrod wasn't sure. He wanted to know what made the noise. But, he couldn't let Leon down.

  B. Jarrod wasn't sure he wanted to know what made the noise, but he couldn't let Leon down.

  C. Jarrod wasn't sure he wanted to know. What made the noise? But, he couldn't let Leon down.

  D. Jarrod wasn't sure. He wanted to know what made the noise, but he couldn't let Leon down.

6. What change, if any, is needed in the sentences in lines 16-17 ("They...homer.")?

  A. They were best friends. Besides, maybe the next time it would be his turn to hit the homer.

  B. They were best friends besides. Maybe, the next time it would be his turn to hit the homer.

  C. They were best friends besides. Maybe the next time it would be his turn. To hit the homer.

  D. Make no change.

Your Turn 5

Write a short story about a situation that involves two friends. Your story may be something that actually happened to you and a friend or to two people you know. But, it can also be fictional. A fictional story is one that is invented by your imagination. It can be based upon something that may have happened or may be true, but it doesn't have to be.

After you have completed the first draft of your story, be sure to read it carefully for any possible revisions that may be needed.

Explanations for "Marissa Writes to Juanita" (Pg. 46):

1. The answer is **C**.

    Choice A is not correct. This sentence conveys the idea that Marissa was excited at getting the phone call when she was really excited about getting the lead in the play.

    Choice B is not correct. This sentence does not contain the important detail that she got the lead in the play.

    Choice C is correct. It contains all of the key elements of the two sentences.

    Choice D is not the best answer. It does not tell how Marissa learned that she got the lead in the play.

2. The answer is **C**.

    Choice A is incorrect. The subject is plural, so the plural form of the verb is needed.

    Choice B is incorrect. The word **girls** is just a plural noun, not a plural possesssive noun.

    Choice C is correct. The adverbial form of the word **sure** is needed in this sentence.

    Choice D is incorrect because a change is needed in this sentence.

3. The answer is **B**.

    Choice A is incorrect. This is not a direct quotation that requires quotation marks.

    Choice B is correct. What is needed is parallel construction of the verb phrases: *to sing*, *to dance*, and *to do* acrobatics.

    Choice C is incorrect. The comma after **people** is incorrect. It changes the sentence structure.

    Choice D is incorrect because a revision is needed in the sentence.

4. The answer is **A**.

    Choice A is correct. The correct spelling of the word needed in this sentence is **know**, the verb.

    Choice B is incorrect. In the past tense of the verb **study**, the **y** changes to **i** before the **-ed** is added.

    Choice C is incorrect. The word **past** refers to time gone by. The word **passed** is a verb form with many meanings, including the ideas **to go**, or **to move forward, through,** or **out**. None of these meanings fit the meaning of the sentence.

    Choice D is incorrect because a change is needed.

5. The answer is **D**.

   Choice A is incorrect. This sentence is not the best way to combine the ideas contained in the sentences because it merely strings the sentences together with the use of **and**s.

   Choice B is not correct. While two points are combined into one sentence, the third point is in a separate sentence.

   Choice C is incorrect. This is somewhat like the first choice. The phrases are linked by **and**s.

   Choice D is correct. This sentence effectively combines the ideas expressed in the three sentences.

6. The answer is **B**.

   Choice A is not correct. The word **director** doesn't require a capital letter.

   Choice B is correct. The pronoun **they** is plural and requires a plural verb form.

   Choice C is incorrect. In this sentence the adjective is correct. The comparative form is not needed.

   Choice D is incorrect because a change is needed.

7. The answer is **D**.

   Choice A is incorrect. The verb **told** is correct. **Tolled** refers to the sound made by the ringing of bells.

   Choice B is not correct. The correct form is the verb **hear**, not the adverb **here**.

   Choice C is incorrect. The word **week** indicating a period of time is correct, rather than the adjective **weak**, meaning "lack of strength."

   Choice D is correct. No change is needed.

8. The answer is **D**.

   Choice A is incorrect. The singular pronoun requires the singular verb form.

   Choice B is not correct because **surprise** is spelled correctly.

   Choice C is not correct because the word **director** does not require a capital letter.

   Choice D is correct. No change is needed.

Explanations for "Letter to the Principal" (Pg. 49):

1. The correct form of the verb **happen** in this sentence is **happened**. The action occurred in the past.

2. The correct verb form should be the past tense of the verb **start, started**.

3. a. One choice is to make two sentences:

   Mr. Hamilton told us we would have to define 25 words and use each of them in a sentence. We would have to answer character and plot questions about novels we have read this year.

   b. Another choice is to make a compound sentence:

   Mr. Hamilton told us we would have to define 25 words and use each of them in a sentence, and we would have to answer questions about plot and character in the novels we have read this year.

   c. A third choice is to include all of the ideas in one sentence using a colon before the list of items:

   Mr. Hamilton told us we would do all of the following: define 25 words, use each in a sentence, and answer plot and character questions about novels we have read.

4. The word **okay** is an unclear word that could be changed. The choices might include: **fine, all right, not a problem, not a concern**, or similar completions. The feeling being conveyed is that the writer, and perhaps other students, felt confident in what they expected would be included on the test.

5. One way of combining the sentences would be:

   Even the questions about the novels were different because we were asked to compare the themes of two novels and to describe how the main characters would act in three different situations.

   Another revision could be to leave the first sentence as is and combine the next two sentences into one sentence:

   Even the questions about the novels were different. We were asked to compare the themes of two novels and to describe how the main characters would act in three different situations.

6. The correct word is **fair**, not **fare**. The concern of the writer is that something was unjust. The teacher had told the students what to expect on the test and that didn't happen. The spelling **fare** often refers to the cost of transportation. **Fair** refers to justice.

7. The sentence in line 19 can be deleted: "We don't like to take tests, usually." This sentence does not add any important information to the content.

8. A good transitional word to begin paragraph 4 would be **afterwards** or **then**.

Explanations for "Dear Senator" (Pg. 52):

1. The correct word is **there**, the adverb, not **their**, because **their** is a possessive pronoun that must modify a noun. It cannot stand alone. Furthermore, it does not fit the meaning of the sentence.

2. One way of combining the sentences is:

   Our schools collect food and clothing for needy families, and our churches have food pantries and soup kitchens for hungry people.

3. One way to combine the sentences is:

   They can't help it if their parents aren't together, their apartments burned down, and their parents can't find an affordable apartment.

4. The word to join the sentences could be the conjunction **but**. **However** could also be used. The punctuation would be different for these two words. If **but** were used, there would be a comma after **home** and **they** would be written with a lower case letter. If **however** were used, there would be a semicolon after **home**, a comma after **however**, and **they** would be written with a lower case letter.

5. The sentence in line 16, "Many people own their own homes," can be deleted. It isn't relevant in this context.

Explanations for "A Game of Stickball" (Pg. 54):

1. The answer is **C**.

> **Choice A** is incorrect. This choice contains sentence fragments. "In a vacant lot" and "Not too far from their apartment house" are not sentences.

> **Choice B** is incorrect. This choice contains a sentence fragment. "In a vacant lot not too far from their apartment house" is not a sentence. Students shouldn't be deceived into thinking that a long collection of words constitutes a complete sentence.

> **Choice C** is correct. This is a complete sentence. It combines the sentence and the fragment that appear in lines 1-2 of the text.

> **Choice D** is incorrect since a change is needed in the text.

2. The answer is **A**.

> **Choice A** combines the sentence with the fragment to make one complete sentence.

> **Choice B through D** all contain sentence fragments rather than one complete sentence.

3. The answer is **B**.

> **Choice A** is incorrect. It contains a sentence fragment, "At Leon's amazing hit."

> **Choice B** is correct. The run-on sentence in lines 4-5 should be divided to correct this problem. One way is to make it into two sentences by using a period after **hit**, and capitalizing **it**.

> **Choice C** is incorrect. It could be a correct choice if the pronoun **it** was not included in the second sentence.

> **Choice D** is incorrect. A comma is not the proper punctuation to separate the two sentences. If a semicolon had been used, that would have made this a correct choice.

4. The answer is **D**.

> **Choice A** is incorrect. "With bases loaded that cleared the center field wall" is not a complete sentence.

> **Choice B** is incorrect. "That cleared the center field wall" is not a complete sentence.

> **Choice C** is incorrect. The sentences do not convey the intention of the writer in the passage.

> **Choice D** is correct. No change is needed. The sentence is long, but it is the best choice.

5. The answer is **B**.

    Choices A, C, and **D** are all sentences, but they are not in keeping with the content of the text. Sentences may be correct, but they also need to make sense in the passage.

    Choice B is correct. The sentence needs a comma to separate the two combined sentences.

6. The answer is **A**.

    Choice A is correct. The run-on sentence needs a period after **friends**. A comma is needed after the word **besides** because it is an introductory word.

    Choice B is incorrect. This is a poor way to divide the run-on sentence to make two sentences.

    Choice C is incorrect. This choice contains a sentence fragment.

    Choice D is incorrect because a change is needed.

C. Summary

    In this chapter, you have practiced different revising skills using different types of writing texts. In Section A, you reviewed four different types of writing. In Section B, you practiced these types using four different selections. The first was a piece of writing that was written to a friend or relative. This might be categorized as writing to "entertain." The second piece was written to a school official about a school-related matter. This text comes under the heading of being informational. The third piece was written to a public official for the purpose of persuading the individual to take some action you desire on a topic. Finally, the last piece was typical of the writing you do in school as homework or class assignments in various disciplines. This example is typical of English assignments you may be given.

    This chapter offered you opportunities to practice types of revisions. Revising a text is an important stage in the writing process before you can produce a final draft.

    In the next chapter, you will be given activities that will ask you to edit texts to correct other types of possible errors in both the first draft and the final draft of your writing.

CHAPTER FIVE

Practice in Editing Sentence Structure

After you have revised the text by reorganizing it, the last stage needed to complete a final draft is editing. Editing includes checking for spelling, punctuation, and capitalization errors. In addition, you need to see if you have made any grammatical errors. As part of your English classes, your teachers spend a lot of time on these types of mechanical editing errors. You encountered some of them in Chapter 4.

In this chapter, we will concentrate on a specific type of sentence structure editing problem that seems to occur in much student writing. These errors involve incomplete sentences, run-on sentences, or sentences that could be combined to form better or more interesting sentences. You were introduced to some of these concepts in the previous chapter; here, they are fully explained for you. You will also be given the opportunity to practice these skills.

A. Incomplete Sentences

An incomplete sentence is sometimes referred to as a sentence fragment. As the name implies, the group of words is only a part of a sentence. Something is missing. A correction is needed to make it a complete sentence. A sentence fragment or incomplete sentence may be caused by a lack of a predicate or the lack of a subject or both.

To illustrate an incomplete sentence or sentence fragment, consider these examples.

1. **Hiking in the woods.**

   This is an incomplete sentence because we don't know who is hiking in the woods. There is no predicate or subject for the sentence.

   We can correct the sentence fragment in many ways. Here are two suggestions.

   Ivan was hiking in the woods.

   Hiking in the woods gave Manuel a chance to study the forest undergrowth.

2. **The first signs of winter.**

> This is an incomplete sentence because there is no verb. We can make it a complete sentence by adding a verb or a verb and more information.

> **The first signs of winter were the cool winds that began blowing from the northwest.**

> We could add a subject and verb to make a complete sentence.

> **Migrating birds are the first signs of winter.**

> **TIP:** ✓ *Don't be fooled by the number of words in a sentence. Just because there are a lot of words does not mean something is a complete sentence.*

3. **Willie ran.**

> This is a sentence. However, the following groups of words are not:

> **Why Willie ran.**

> **Running after the bus that was pulling away from the curb.**

> The thoughts in these two fragments can be combined to form complete sentences.

> **Willie ran after the bus that was pulling away from the curb.**
> *or*
> **Running after the bus that was pulling away from the curb, Willie stumbled and fell.**
> *or*
> **Why Willie ran after the bus that was pulling away from the curb, no one knew.**

B. Run-on Sentences

In a run-on sentence, the writer has linked together what should be two sentences without a proper punctuation mark. The run-on sentences can be separated by placing a period between them and beginning the second sentence with a capital letter, or the two sentences can be separated by a semicolon. If the semicolon is used, the two sentences should be closely linked in what they express.

> **Martha was running an errand for her mother she had a grocery list and ten dollars in her pocket.**

This is a run-on sentence. It can be corrected either by placing a period after *mother* and capitalizing *she*, or by placing a semicolon after *mother*. Because the two ideas are closely related, either correction is appropriate.

Now, let's look at a slightly different situation.

Martha was running an errand for her mother while she was at the store she met a friend and they decided to get an ice cream cone.

This is also a run-on sentence; however, the ideas are somewhat different in the two sentences. In this case, a period after *mother* would be a better choice than a semicolon. Additional corrections will be needed in the second sentence. The word *while* will need a capital letter. A comma will be needed after the word *store*. A comma will be needed after the word *friend* because this is two sentences joined by the conjunction *and*.

C. Sentence Combining

Another type of editing error involves joining ideas to form a better sentence. It is called sentence combining. Some writers tend to use many short sentences in their writing. Frequently, some of these short sentences can be put together to make longer and more interesting reading.

Morgan had a dog. His dog was friendly. His dog wouldn't bark at Morgan's friends. He would bark at other dogs.

Here we see several short sentences about Morgan's dog. We might be able to combine them into a single sentence that could improve the text.

Morgan's dog was friendly and never barked at Morgan's friends; however, it would bark at other dogs.

or

Morgan's dog would bark at other dogs, but not at Morgan's friends.

D. Practice Passages

Now you will have the opportunity to edit some short selections. The errors may be incomplete sentences, run-on sentences, choices of ways to combine sentences, or some sentences that require no correction. These activities will give you practice in applying your editing skills to pieces of writing by other authors. Often, it is easier to find errors in the works of others than it is in our own writing. Explanations that will help you recognize why an answer is correct or incorrect appear at the end of the chapter. First, answer the questions without referring to the explanations; then, review your answers with those provided.

Decide if any changes are needed. If so, select the best of the four choices to correct the problem.

Passage A: King Arthur

1   The ruins of Glastonbury Abbey may hold the secrets of King

2   Arthur. They may be where Excalibur is. They may be where the Holy

3   Grail is hidden. The legend of King Arthur is one that has captured the

4   imagination of people. Through tales, plays, and even Hal Foster's car-

5   toon strip, "Prince Valiant." Queen Guinevere, Merlin the magician, Sir

6   Lancelot, and Sir Gawain are familiar persons associated with Arthur.

7   Included in the Arthurian tales are accounts of Arthur's sword,

8   Excalibur, and the Knights of the Round Table's search for the Holy

9   Grail.

10   A beautiful area in western England has been suggested as the

11   burial place of Arthur and Guinevere this is Glastonbury. During the

12   rebuilding of an abbey at Glastonbury in A.D. 1184, the monks uncov-

13   ered a cross containing an inscription. That when translated said,

14   "Here lies buried the renowned King Arthur of the Isle of Avalon."

15   There is no conclusive proof that the remains they uncovered there are

16   those of Arthur and Guinevere, but in 1278, the bones were placed in a

17   marble tomb and buried in front of the new church altar.

1. Which is the best way if any, to revise sentences 1-3 ("The...hidden.")?

   A. The Glastonbury Abbey is ruined and it may be where King Arthur and Excalibur and the Holy Grail are.

   B. The Glastonbury Abbey was ruined by King Arthur and the Excalibur. The Holy Grail is hidden there.

   C. The ruins of Glastonbury Abbey may hold the secrets of what happened to King Arthur, Excalibur, and the Holy Grail.

   D. Glastonbury Abbey is an important ruin to King Arthur and the Holy Grail.

2. What is the best way, if any, to revise the sentences in lines 3-5 ("The...Valiant.")?

   A. The legend of King Arthur is one that has captured the imagination of people through tales and plays. And even Hal Foster's cartoon strip, "Prince Valiant."

   B. The legend of King Arthur is one; that has captured the imagination of people. Through tales, plays, and even Hal Foster's cartoon strip, "Prince Valiant."

   C. The legend of King Arthur is one that has captured the imagination of people through tales, plays, and even Hal Foster's cartoon strip, "Prince Valiant."

   D. The legend of King Arthur appears in many forms of literature.

3. What is the best way to revise the sentences in lines 7-9 ("Included...Grail.")?

   A. Included in the Arthurian tales are accounts, of Arthur's sword, Excalibur; and the Knights of the Round Table's search for the Holy Grail.

   B. Included in the Arthurian tales are accounts of Arthur's sword. And the Knights of the Round Table's search for the Holy Grail.

   C. Included in the Arthurian tales are accounts of Arthur's Excalibur, the Knights of the Round Table's search for the Holy Grail.

   D. Make no change.

4. What is the best revision of lines 10-11 ("A...Glastonbury.")?

   A. A beautiful area in Western England. Has been suggested as the burial place of Arthur and Guinevere, this is Glastonbury.

   B. A beautiful area in western England has been suggested as the burial place of Arthur and Guinevere; this is Glastonbury.

   C. A beautiful place in western England has been suggested for the burial place of Arthur and Guinevere, Glastonbury.

   D. A beautiful area is Glastonbury. The burial place of King Arthur and Guinevere.

5. Which is the best revision of lines 11-14
   ("During...Avalon.")?

    A. During the rebuilding of an abbey
       at Glastonbury in A.D. 1184, the
       monks uncovered a cross; that
       when translated said, "Here lies
       buried the renowned King Arthur
       of the Isle of Avalon."

    B. During the rebuilding of an abbey
       at Glastonbury in A.D. 1184, the
       monks uncovered a cross that
       said, "Here lies buried the
       renowned King Arthur of the Isle
       of Avalon."

    C. During the rebuilding of an abbey
       at Glastonbury in A.D. 1184, the
       monks uncovered a cross contain-
       ing an inscription that when
       translated said, "Here lies buried
       the renowned King Arthur of the
       Isle of Avalon."

    D. A Glastonbury cross, discovered
       in A.D. 1184, had the inscription
       "Here lies buried the renowned
       King Arthur of the Isle of
       Avalon."

Read the report about Big Bend National Park. Choose the best sentence revision, if needed, to improve the content.

Passage B: Big Bend National Park

1   One of our largest and most spectacular national parks is in the
2   western part of Texas it is Big Bend National Park. The name aptly
3   describes how the Rio Grande River changes course and cuts through
4   the mountains. To form beautiful canyons.

5   This park has desert land. It has volcanos. It has forests. It has
6   such a wonderful ecosystem that it has been designated an
7   International Biosphere Reserve. There are only about 250 of these
8   reserves in the entire world.

9   Within the park one can find a range of climates. This is
10   because of the differences in altitudes and in the amount of precipita-
11   tion. Some mountains are over 7,800 feet high and may get snow
12   during the winter months. While other areas near the Rio Grande are
13   only 1800 feet above sea level. And this desert area gets only about 6
14   inches of rainfall each year.

15   This vast area is home to more than 75 species of mammals,
16   many reptiles and amphibians, and a variety of fish, insects, and
17   arachnids. Big Bend attracts more than 400 species of birds, which is
18   more than any other national park in the United States or Canada.

19   Obviously, in a place bigger than the state of Rhode Island,
20   there is a lot to see. However, this park receives only about 250,000 vis-
21   itors per year. Compared to about 4 million who visit the Grand
22   Canyon National Park. Or the over 3 million who go to Yosemite
23   National Park each year.

1. What is the best revision for the sentence in lines 1-2 ("One...Park.")?

   A. One of our largest and most spectacular national parks is Big Bend National Park.

   B. One of our largest and most spectacular national parks is in the western part of Texas, it is Big Bend National Park.

   C. One of our largest and most spectacular national parks is in the western part of Texas: Big Bend National Park.

   D. Big Bend is a national park in Texas.

2. What is the best revision for the sentences in lines 2-4 ("The...canyons.")?

   A. The name aptly describes how the Rio Grande River changes course and cuts through the mountains to form beautiful canyons.

   B. The name describes how the Rio Grande River cuts through the mountains to form canyons.

   C. The name aptly describes how the Rio Grande River changes course and cuts through the mountains; to form beautiful canyons.

   D. Make no change.

3. What is the best revision of the sentences in line 5 ("This...forests.")?

   A. This park has desert land, it has volcanos, it has forests.

   B. This park has desert land, volcanos, and forests.

   C. This park has desert land with volcanos and forests.

   D. Parks may have forests, deserts, or volcanoes.

4. What is the best revision of the sentences in lines 11-14 ("Some...year.")?

   A. Some mountains are over 7,800 feet. They may get snow during the winter months. While other areas near the Rio Grande are only 1800 feet above sea level. The desert gets only 6 inches of rainfall each year.

   B. Some mountains are over 7,800 feet and may get snow during the winter months, while other areas near the Rio Grande are only 1800 feet above sea level. And the desert gets only about 6 inches of rainfall each year.

   C. Some mountains are over 7,800 feet and may get snow during the winter months, while desert areas near the Rio Grande are only 1800 feet above sea level and receive only 6 inches of rainfall each year.

   D. Some mountains over 7,000 feet are snow covered in winters.

5. What is the best revision for the sentence in lines 17-18 ("Big...species.")?

    A. Big Bend attracts many more species of birds then any other park.

    B. Big Bend attracts more species of birds than any other park. More than 400 species of birds.

    C. Big Bend attracts more species of birds than any other national park in the United States or Canada. More than 400 species.

    D. Make no change.

6. What is the best revision for the sentences in lines 20-23 ("However...year.")?

    A. However, this park receives only about 250,000 visitors, compared to the 4 million who visit the Grand Canyon National Park and the over 3 million who go to Yosemite National Park.

    B. However, this park receives only about 250,000 visitors. Compared to about 4 million who visit the Grand Canyon and over 3 million who visit Yosemite.

    C. However, this park receives only about 250,000 visitors; compared to about 4 million who visit the Grand Canyon National Park and 3 million who visit Yosemite National Park.

    D. However, there are several parks that receive many millions of visitors.

Read the article and decide what corrections are needed.

Passage C: Miniaturization

1   While many people are concerned with "the big picture" of our

2   world and of our universe. There are scientists who are focusing on

3   small items. These individuals are busy creating miniature robots they

4   are developing micromotors the size of a speck of dust.

5   The silicone industry is on the verge of finding many uses for

6   microscopic sensors. This technology has applications for space explo-

7   ration. It has applications for delicate surgery. It has uses in ecology

8   and in the handling of hazardous materials.

9   Some major American companies are engaged in this micro-

10   technology. They believe it holds promise for the automotive industry;

11   for monitoring patients during surgery; for improving athletic perfor-

12   mance in golf, rowing, and scuba diving. Using this technology, some

13   companies have already manufactured ballpoint pens that can detect

14   forgeries.

15   The possibilities of reducing the size of silicone chips. While at

16   the same time increasing computer memory. Are only beginning to

17   be explored. Future technology may make it possible to have

18   machines do both the highly dangerous work and the repetitive,

19   boring tasks independent of direct human involvement.

1. Which of the following choices is the best revision of the sentences in lines 1-3 ("While...items.")?

   A. While many people are concerned with "the big picture" of our world and of our universe; there are scientists who are focusing on small items.

   B. While many people are concerned with "the big picture," of our world and of our universe. There are scientists who are focusing on small items.

   C. While many people are concerned with "the big picture" of our world and of our universe, there are scientists who are focusing on small items.

   D. While some people are concerned with "the big picture," others are not.

2. Which of the following choices is the best revision of the sentence in lines 3-4 ("These...dust.")?

   A. These individuals are busy creating miniature robots that are developing micromotors the size of a speck of dust.

   B. These individuals are busy creating miniature robots; they are developing micromotors the size of a speck of dust.

   C. These individuals are busy creating. Miniature robots they are developing micromotors the size of a speck of dust.

   D. Micromotors the size of specks of dust are in miniature robots.

3. What is the best revision of the sentences in lines 6-8 ("This...materials.")?

   A. This technology has applications for space exploration. It has applications for delicate surgery, it has uses in ecology. It can be used in handling hazardous materials.

   B. This technology has applications for space exploration; it has applications for delicate surgery. It has uses in ecology and in the handling of hazardous materials.

   C. This technology has applications for space exploration, for delicate surgery, for uses in ecology, and for the handling of hazardous materials.

   D. This technology is important and has many applications in science.

4. Which of the following choices is the best revision of the sentences in lines 10-12 ("They...diving.")?

   A. They believe it holds promise for the automotive industry. For the monitoring of patients during surgery. And for improving athletic performance in golf, rowing, and scuba diving.

   B. They believe it holds promise. For the automotive industry. For the monitoring of patients during surgery. And for improving athletic performance in golf, rowing, and scuba diving.

   C. They believe it holds promise for many areas: the automotive industry; the monitoring of patients during surgery; and the improvement of athletic performance in golf, rowing, and scuba diving.

   D. They believe it will help the automotive industry, patients, and athletes.

5. Which of the following choices is the best revision of lines 15-17 ("The...explored.")?

   A. The possibilities of reducing the size of silicone chips while at the same time increasing computer memory are only beginning to be explored.

   B. The possibilities of reducing the size of silicone chips while at the same time increasing computer memory, are only beginning to be explored.

   C. The possibilities of reducing the size of silicone chips; while at the same time increasing computer memory are only beginning to be explored.

   D. The possibilities of reducing the size of silicone chips, while at the same time increasing computer memory, are only beginning to be explored.

Read the article and answer the questions.

Passage D: Bats

1   Have you ever heard someone referred to as "having bats in the

2   belfry"? This expression has come to mean that the person acts in a

3   strange way. The phrase probably began when people noticed bats.

4   Flying around churchyards. And belfry towers. Searching for food.

5   This is just one of many negative references associated with

6   bats. In reality, bats are very beneficial mammals they can be found

7   wherever there are large quantities of insects. They can consume

8   enough insects in a single night to increase their weight by up to 50

9   percent.

10   These mammals are misunderstood. Partly, because of some

11   books and films that have been produced. Showing them as blood-

12   sucking vampires. The reason why bats have been seen flying with

13   their mouths open and teeth bared is because they must fly with their

14   mouths open to keep from bumping into objects. This is part of their

15   echo location system. However, this picture of the bat has frightened

16   many people.

17   Those who study bats tell us that they represent about one-fourth

18   of the mammals of the world. There are about 800 species of small

19   bats, microbats. They vary greatly in features and habits. Many are

20   becoming extinct. Bats play an important role in our ecology. As

21   people become more knowledgeable about these mammals, they

22   may put aside their fears of these basically gentle animals.

1. What is the best revision for lines 3-4 ("The...food.")?

   A. The phrase probably began, when people noticed bats. Flying around churchyards and belfry towers. Searching for food.

   B. The phrase probably began when people noticed bats flying around churchyards and belfry towers searching for food.

   C. The phrase probably began when people noticed bats flying around churchyards, and belfry towers searching for food.

   D. The phrase probably began when people noticed bats, flying around churchyards and belfry towers, searching for food.

2. What is the best revision for lines 6-7 ("In...insects.")?

   A. In reality, bats are very beneficial mammals, they can be found wherever there are large quantities of insects.

   B. In reality, bats are very beneficial. Mammals, they can be found wherever there are large quantities of insects.

   C. In reality, bats are very beneficial mammals; they can be found wherever there are large quantities of insects.

   D. Whenever there are insects, there are beneficial bats in the area.

3. What is the best revision for lines 10-12 ("These...vampires.")?

   A. These mammals are misunderstood partly because of some books and films that have been produced showing them as blood-sucking vampires.

   B. These mammals are misunderstood partly because of some books and films. That have been produced showing them as blood-sucking vampires.

   C. These mammals are misunderstood. Partly, because of some books and films that have been produced, showing them as blood-sucking vampires.

   D. Bats are not understood by people.

4. What is the best revision for lines 18-20 ("There...ecology.")?

   A. There are 800 species of extinct microbats that are important to our ecology.

   B. Some of the 800 species of small bats, or microbats, which vary greatly in features and habits, are becoming extinct. All bats are important to our ecology.

   C. Microbats are important to our ecology; but they are different in features and habits and are becoming extinct.

   D. Many of the 800 species of microbats that vary in features and habits, are becoming extinct.

Explanation for "King Arthur"(Pg. 66):

1. The answer is **C**.

> **Choice A** is incorrect. The sentence is awkward.

> **Choice B** is incorrect. These sentences aren't in keeping with the content of the text.

> **Choice C** is correct. This sentence contains all of the key elements of the three sentences in the text.

> **Choice D** is incorrect. This sentence doesn't contain all of the information from the three sentences in the text.

2. The answer is **C**.

> **Choice A** is incorrect. This choice does not contain two complete sentences.

> **Choice B** is incorrect. This choice contains several errors. The first sentence is not a compound sentence separated by a semicolon. The second fragment is not a complete sentence.

> **Choice C** is correct. This is a complete sentence that includes all of the data from the sentence.

> **Choice D** is incorrect. This sentence is not as clear or as specific as Choice C.

3. The answer is **D**.

> **Choice A** is incorrect. The punctuation interferes with the construction of the sentence.

> **Choice B** is incorrect. This is not two complete sentences. "And the Knights of the Round Table's search for the Holy Grail" is a sentence fragment, not a sentence.

> **Choice C** is incorrect. This is not a smoothly-written sentence. A conjunction is needed after **Excalibur**.

> **Choice D** is correct. No change is needed in the text.

4. The answer is **B**.

> **Choice A** is incorrect. This choice contains a fragment and a run-on sentence.

> **Choice B** is correct. The run-on sentence is divided into two sentences separated by a semicolon.

> **Choice C** is incorrect. This sentence does not maintain the intent of the text. It gives the impression that people are looking for someplace to bury Arthur and Guinevere.

> **Choice D** is incorrect. While the first sentence is correct, the second part of the answer is a fragment.

5. The answer is **B**.

> **Choice A** is incorrect. This is not a case where the use of a semicolon is appropriate.

> **Choice B** is incorrect. The missing element in this sentence is that the inscription on the cross had to be translated before people knew what it said.

> **Choice C** is correct. This sentence contains all of the elements present in lines 11-14.

> **Choice D** is incorrect. This is true, but it doesn't contain all of the key points from lines 11-14.

Explanation for "Big Bend National Park"(Pg. 69):

1. The answer is **C**.

> **Choice A** is incorrect. It fails to tell the location of the park.

> **Choice B** is incorrect. This is actually two sentences, so the comma is not the needed punctuation mark.

> **Choice C** is correct. This sentence contains all of the data from lines 1-2 and is punctuated correctly.

> **Choice D** is incorrect. This answer doesn't describe key elements of the park.

2. The answer is **A**.

>   **Choice A** is correct. This choice combines the sentence and the fragment into a complete sentence.

>   **Choice B** is incorrect. Choice A is more descriptive of the canyons than this sentence is.

>   **Choice C** is incorrect. The semicolon is not needed in this sentence. "To form beautiful canyons" is not a sentence.

>   **Choice D** is incorrect because a change is needed in the text.

3. The answer is **B**.

>   **Choice A** is incorrect. This is a series of sentences without proper punctuation between them.

>   **Choice B** is correct. This sentence effectively combines the ideas expressed in line 5.

>   **Choice C** is incorrect. The sense is not correctly expressed in this sentence. The volcanoes and forests are in the park, but they are not necessarily in the desert.

>   **Choice D** is incorrect. This may be true, but it doesn't directly relate to Big Bend.

4. The answer is **C**.

>   **Choice A** is incorrect. There is a sentence fragment, "While other areas near the Rio Grande are only 1800 feet above sea level," in this choice of answer.

>   **Choice B** is incorrect. The final sentence is poorly constructed. It begins with an **and**. Moreover, it should be connected to the idea of the altitude above sea level.

>   **Choice C** is correct. This sentence contains all of the key points contained in lines 11-14 and corrects the fragments.

>   **Choice D** is incorrect. This answer lacks many key elements of the text.

5. The answer is **D**.

 Choice A is incorrect. This sentence is inaccurate. We know only that this park attracts more birds than other national parks in the United States and Canada. There may be other national parks in other countries that attract more species of birds.

 Choice B is incorrect. This answer contains inaccurate data and an incorrect division of the text into one sentence and one fragment.

 Choice C is incorrect. This is not two sentences.

 Choice D is correct. The sentence is correct as it stands.

6. The answer is **A**.

 Choice A is correct. All of the data is contained within a single sentence.

 Choice B is incorrect. This choice contains a sentence and a fragment.

 Choice C is incorrect. The semicolon is not the correct punctuation for in this sentence.

 Choice D is incorrect. This is true, but it doesn't include all of the facts contained in lines 20-23.

Explanations for "Miniaturization" (Pg. 72):

1. The answer is **C**.

 Choice A is incorrect. The semicolon is not the correct punctuation needed.

 Choice B is incorrect. This choice contains a fragment and a sentence. "While many people are concerned with 'the big picture' of our world and of our universe" is a fragment.

 Choice C is correct. The comma is the correct punctuation in this case.

 Choice D is incorrect. This answer doesn't contain all of the data in lines 1-3 of the text.

2. The answer is **B**.

 Choice A is incorrect. This choice does not accurately reflect the ideas expressed in the text.

 Choice B is correct. The two sentences are separated by a semicolon. If the choice had separated the two sentences with a period, that would have been correct, too.

 Choice C is incorrect. This choice contains a fragment.

 Choice D is incorrect. It does not contain accurate information.

3. The answer is **C**.

Choice **A** is incorrect. This choice contains a run-on sentence. It doesn't adequately combine the ideas into revised sentences.

Choice **B** is incorrect. The sentences do combine data; however, this is not the most effective revision of the text.

Choice **C** is correct. This sentence combines all of the date in lines 6-8 into an effective sentence.

Choice **D** is incorrect. This sentence is too general to be the best choice for revising the text.

4. The answer is **C**.

Choice **A** is incorrect. This choice contains sentence fragments rather than a complete sentence or sentences.

Choice **B** is incorrect. Again, this choice contains sentence fragments rather than a complete sentence.

Choice **C** is correct. This sentence contains all of the data from lines 10-12 of the text, correctly punctuated.

Choice **D** is incorrect. This sentence does not present the information properly. Therefore, it is not the best revision of the text.

5. The answer is **A**.

Choice **A** is correct. This choice combines the fragments in the text into a meaningful, complete sentence.

Choice **B** is incorrect. The comma separates the subject from the verb.

Choice **C** is incorrect. The semicolon is not needed in the sentence.

Choice **D** is incorrect. The phrase is important to the subject of the sentence and should not be separated by commas.

Explanations for "Bats" (Pg. 75):

1. The answer is **B**.

> **Choice A** is incorrect. The comma isn't needed after **began**. The other groups of words are fragments, not complete sentences.

> **Choice B** is correct. All of the fragments can be joined to form one sentence. Because the reference to the churchyard and the belfry towers is important to the meaning of the sentence, no internal punctuation is needed in the sentence.

> **Choice C** is incorrect. The comma is not needed after **churchyard**. This is not an example of two sentences being joined by **and**.

> **Choice D** is incorrect. The reference to bats flying around churchyards and belfry towers is relevant to comprehending the text and should not be separated by commas.

2. The answer is **C**.

> **Choice A** is incorrect. A comma is not the appropriate punctuation to separate the run-on sentence.

> **Choice B** is incorrect. This is not the best way to revise the text. The noun, **mammals**, should be included in the first sentence.

> **Choice C** is correct. The semicolon is the correct punctuation to use in this revision. A period could have been used in place of the semicolon, and that would have been correct, too.

> **Choice D** is incorrect. The content is not precisely correct according to the text.

3. The answer is **A**.

> **Choice A** is correct. The sentence in line 10 can be joined with the rest of the concepts from lines 11-12 to form a single sentence.

> **Choice B** is incorrect. This contains a sentence and a fragment.

> **Choice C** is incorrect. Again, there is a sentence and a fragment in this revision.

> **Choice D** is incorrect. The sentence is correct, but it does not contain sufficient data from the text.

4. The answer is **B**.

   Choice A is incorrect. This sentence revision contains inaccurate data.

   Choice B is correct. Much of the data from the text can be combined into one sentence. However, some of the data is best left to form a second sentence.

   Choice C is incorrect. The punctuation is incorrect. In addition, the idea that all bats are important to our ecology has not been included in this revision.

   Choice D is incorrect. The punctuation is incorrect. A comma would be needed after bats. In addition, no mention is made of the importance of all bats to your ecology.

CHAPTER SIX

Practicing Writing and Revising

In this chapter, you will be given opportunities to practice the types of writing activities that you might expect to find on a standardized or state writing test. You will be given writing prompts to be used in writing tasks. In addition, you will be given several pieces of written material to revise and edit.

Before we begin these activities, let's look briefly at the writing process and the scoring of essays that are involved in these types of tests. When you are writing an essay on these tests, you will not have enough time to use the complete writing process. You will be producing only a first draft of an essay. This means that you will use your pre-writing strategies and your editing and revising skills to a limited degree; but, you will not receive feedback or suggestions on how to improve your writing or be able to rewrite your essay.

A. Scoring Essays

Probably when you write essays in class or for homework your teachers give you a numerical or letter grade indicating how well they think you have completed the assignment. Another way to score your writing is to receive a point score for your essay. The scores may be on a scale of 1 to 4. Just like the numerical score or letter grade, the lower point scores indicate writings that are not of high quality and the higher point scores indicate the better writing pieces. Usually, your essay will need a point score at the average range for it to be considered acceptable.

When you submit your writing assignments to your classroom teachers, they will frequently indicate where you have made errors of spelling, punctuation, and grammar. In fact, they may base most of your grade on

how few of these errors your writing contains. They may or may not give you feedback on what they thought about how you organized your ideas or what you had to say. However, on standardized or state writing tests, the readers are more interested in the content and organization of the material than they are in the mechanics. This doesn't mean that you will receive a high score for an essay that contains many errors, but it does mean that having a few mistakes will not lower your score severely. For instance, if the reader thought your paper dealt effectively with the topic, was well-organized, was worthy of a score of 5, and had two or three minor errors, you would receive the 5. If your paper was worth a 5 on content and organization, but you had five or six errors, then the paper could be downgraded to a 4.

In our view, it makes good sense to give greater weight to the content and organization of a paper than to the mechanics. However, this means that the writer must give greater attention to the pre-writing stage of the writing process and carefully consider the content of the piece of writing. If the writer ignores this stage, chances are that the product will suffer from a lack of good content and probably a lack of good organization. It means that time needs to be given to some editing and revising, too. It would be a shame to have a basically good piece of writing receive a lower score because of technical errors that could have easily been corrected by rereading the piece of writing prior to the end of the test.

B. Strategies for Writing Essays

• Read the essay prompt carefully.

• What are you being asked to write about?

• Who is your audience?

• What type of writing is it (narrative, informational, persuasive, etc.)?

• Do not begin writing your essay immediately! Take about 5 minutes to jot down your thoughts on the topic, using an appropriate pre-writing strategy. You can make a map of your ideas, a Venn diagram, an outline, or a list.

Step 1: Read the Prompt

Here is a writing prompt. Read it and take a few minutes to jot down what comes to your mind on the topic.

> People are concerned about animals becoming endangered species. Some people are concerned about the numbers of dolphins that are becoming trapped in fishing nets and are dying.
>
> Write an essay describing why you think this is or is not a problem that should concern us. If you think it is a problem, suggest what you think might be done to solve the problem. If you don't think it is a problem, tell what you might say to those people who believe it is a problem.

You will probably find that you have noted more ideas than you can hope to include in your essay. Select a few key ideas and plan how you will present these in your essay.

Step 2: Use a Pre-Writing Strategy

Of all of the ideas you jotted down, some of them may not relate to the essay topic. Make two lists. On one list write all of your ideas that could be used in writing your essay. On the other list, write the ideas that do not relate to the topic or that you will not use in your essay.

Usually in a pre-writing exercise you will not map your ideas **and** put those ideas into lists. However, we are suggesting that you do both of these things at this time so we can help you organize your essay.

Step 3: Organize

To the left of each of the ideas you wish to include in your essay, write the number of the paragraph in which you think you will use that idea.

Example:

- **Paragraph 1:** Note the key points about the situation/ problem.

- **Paragraph 2:** Tell why you think it is or is not a concern. Support your position. Don't simply state that you think it is or is not a problem.

- **Paragraph 3:** Provide ideas on how you would solve the problem, or provide information on what you would say to those who think it is a problem to try to persuade them that it is not a matter of concern.

Your Turn 1
· · · · · · · · · · · · · · · · · ·

Write an essay on either the topic of the dolphins or on some other subject that may pose a problem to our environment.

REMEMBER:

- *Take time to engage in a pre-writing strategy!*

- *Organize your ideas into paragraphs.*

- *Write your essay.*

- *Reread your essay to check for possible spelling, capitalization, punctuation, or grammatical errors.*

• *Erase, insert, or cross out and change what needs to be corrected.*

• *This is a first draft and readers expect to see papers that contain corrections.*

Your Turn 2

Using all of the strategies we have discussed in this chapter, write an essay on one of the following topics:

Essay Topic A:

Some companies charge high prices for sneakers. Write an essay telling why you think they should or should not charge those prices. Write why you think their sneakers are better or not better than other less expensive brands, and why you would or would not buy one of these brands.

Essay Topic B:

Some students feel awkward or uncomfortable about their physical appearance or something about themselves. What advice would you give to a good friend to help that person feel better about himself or herself?

C. Revising and Editing

The next part of Chapter 6 will give you additional practice in the editing and revising of written materials. Read each of the three passages and answer the questions that follow.

Read this letter and help Sammy make the necessary corrections.

Passage A: Letter to Aunt Mary

1   Dear Aunt Mary,

2   I just recieved your letter inviting me to your house for the

3   months of July and August. It is great to know you and Uncle Guy

4   enjoy having me as much as I enjoy being with you.

5   My problem is that I have sent in my money to go to blackwood

6   riverbay scout camp in July. Recently, I joined the scouts in my town

7   and they have their annual camp-out the second week in July.

8   Everyone is going. The scout master said I would be able to start work

9   on my Second Class badge. I think I should go, especially since I am a

10   new member of the troop.

11   What if I came to your house near the end of July. That would

12   allow me to go to camp and still come to your house for half of July

13   and all of August.

14   Dad and mom have said they could drive me to your house.

15   This would save you from coming east twice in one summer. Just to

16   pick me up and to bring me back.

17   I hope this new time schedule is all right with you. The activities

18   you have planned when I'm at your house sound great. I would really

19   like to do them with you and Uncle Guy. I enjoy doing things on my

20   summer vacations.

21   Let me know as soon as you can about whether I will be able to

22   visit this summer. I sure hope the answer is yes!

23   Your loving nephew,

      Sammy

1. What change, if any, is needed in lines 2-3 ("I...August.")?

    A. Change **recieved** to **received**.

    B. Change **inviting** to **inviteing**.

    C. Change **July and August** to **july and august**.

    D. Make no change.

2. What change, if any, is needed in lines 5-6 ("My...July.")?

    A. Add a comma after **is**.

    B. Change **blackwood river** to **Blackwood River**.

    C. Change **blackwood river boy scout camp** to **Blackwood River Boy Scout Camp**.

    D. Make no change.

3. What change, if any, is needed in lines 6-7 ("Recently...July.")?

    A. Delete the comma after **Recently**.

    B. Change **scouts** to **scout**.

    C. Add a comma after **town**.

    D. Make no change.

4. What change, if any, is needed in lines 8-9 ("The...badge.")?

    A. Change **scout master** to **Scout Master**.

    B. Put a comma after **said** and quotations before **I** and after **badge**.

    C. Change **Second Class** to **second class**.

    D. Make no change.

5. What change, if any, is needed in paragraph 3?

    A. Add a comma after **July** in sentence 2.

    B. Change the period after **July** in sentence 1 to a question mark.

    C. Add a comma after **camp**.

    D. Make no change.

6. What change, if any, is needed in line 14?

    A. Change **Dad and mom** to **Dad and Mom**.

    B. Add a comma after **said** and quotation marks before **they**, capitalizing **They**, and adding quotation marks after **house**.

    C. Add a comma after **said** and quotation marks before **they** and after **house**.

    D. Make no change.

7. What change is needed in lines 14-16 ("Dad...back.")?

    A. Dad and Mom will drive me to your house, so you won't have to make two trips east this summer.

    B. Dad and Mom will drive me to your house, and you can drive me home.

    C. Driving both ways is a lot. Dad and Mom will drive one way.

    D. Dad and Mom will save you a trip by driving me to your house.

In the blanks below, write the answer that you chose and the reasons why you think your choice is correct and the others are not.

1. Which answer did you choose? _____
   Briefly explain why your choice is correct or better than the others.

   _____

2. Which answer did you choose? _____
   Briefly explain why your choice is correct or better than the others.

   _____

3. Which answer did you choose? _____
   Briefly explain why your choice is correct or better than the others.

   _____

4. Which answer did you choose? _____
   Briefly explain why your choice is correct or better than the others.

   _____

5. Which answer did you choose? _____
   Briefly explain why your choice is correct or better than the others.

   _____

6. Which answer did you choose? _____
   Briefly explain why your choice is correct or better than the others.

   _____

7. Which answer did you choose? _____
   Briefly explain why your choice is correct or better than the others.

   _____

Read this letter to Mrs. Jones. Make the corrections needed.

Passage B: Letter to Mrs. Jones

1 Dear Mrs. Jones:

2   I wish to apply for the mother's helper job you advertised in the

3 *Mid-Cape News*. Even though I'm only thirteen. I think you will find

4 that I am qualified for the job. I could come for an interview anytime

5 after school.

6   This past year, our school offered classes in Child Care for sixth

7 graders. I attended all the sessions. There were eight of them. We

8 learned how to feed and dress babies and young children. The

9 instructors also helped us understand how to decide whether

10 something was safe for the child to play with or use. During one class,

11 mothers brought their young children in and we took turns feeding and

12 changing them.

13   I have had experience watching my younger brother and sister.

14 My mother works part-time at the Mid-Cape Hospital. Whenever that

15 happens, she leaves me in charge of my brother and sister until my

16 father gets home. That is usually for an hour, or maybe hour and a

17 half.

18   Waching young children is fun. I enjoy playing with them. I like

19 to see them laugh. I like to help them learn new words. I like to help

20 them learn new skills. I want to go to college to be a teacher. This

21 type of experience will help me learn more about young children.

22   I am home by 3:30 p.m. Our telephone number is 656-7777. I

23   hope to hear from you soon.

24   Sincerely,

          Bethany Parker

25   Bethany Parker

---

1. What change, if any, is needed in lines 2-3 ("I...*News.*")?

    A. Change **mother's** to **mothers**.

    B. Change **mother's** to **Mother's**.

    C. Change **mother's helper** to **Mother's Helper**.

    D. Make no change.

2. What change, if any, is needed in lines 3-4 ("Even...job.")?

    A. Even though I am only thirteen. I think you will find. I am qualified for the job.

    B. Even though I am only thirteen, I think you will find that I am qualified for the job.

    C. I am thirteen, and I am qualified for the job.

    D. Make no change.

3. What change, if any, is needed in lines 6-7 ("This...graders.")?

    A. Change **school** to **School**.

    B. Change **Child Care** to **child care**.

    C. Change **sixth graders** to **Sixth Graders**.

    D. Make no change.

4. What change, if any, is needed in lines 10-12 ("During...them.")?

    A. Delete the comma after **class**.

    B. Add a period after **in** and make **and** capital.

    C. Add a comma after **in**.

    D. Make no change.

5. What is the best way to revise lines 18-20 ("I...skills.")?

   A. I like to play with children and see them laugh. I like to help them learn new words, and I like to help them learn new skills.

   B. I like to play with children, and I enjoy seeing them laugh and help them learn new words and new skills.

   C. I enjoy seeing children: play, laugh, learn new words, and learn new skills.

   D. I enjoy playing with children, seeing them laugh, and helping them learn new words and skills.

6. Which sentence should be deleted?

   A. Line 7 ("I...sessions.")

   B. Line 7 ("There...them.")

   C. Line 14 ("My...Hospital.")

   D. Line 16-17 ("That...half.")

7. What is the best place for lines 4-5 ("I...school.")?

   A. at the end of paragraph 2

   B. at the end of paragraph 3

   C. at the beginning of paragraph 5

   D. Make no change.

8. What change, if any, is needed in line 22 ("I...7777.")?

   A. Add a comma after **home**.

   B. Change **p.m.** to **P.M.**

   C. Change **Our** to **our**.

   D. Make no change.

In the blanks below, write the answer that you chose and the reasons why you think your choice is correct and the others are not.

1. Which answer did you choose? _____
   Briefly explain why your choice is correct or better than the others.

   _____

2. Which answer did you choose? _____
   Briefly explain why your choice is correct or better than the others.

   _____

3. Which answer did you choose? _____
   Briefly explain why your choice is correct or better than the others.

   _____

4. Which answer did you choose? _____
   Briefly explain why your choice is correct or better than the others.

   _____

5. Which answer did you choose? _____
   Briefly explain why your choice is correct or better than the others.

   _____

6. Which answer did you choose? _____
   Briefly explain why your choice is correct or better than the others.

   _____

7. Which answer did you choose? _____
   Briefly explain why your choice is correct or better than the others.

   _____

8. Which answer did you choose? _____
   Briefly explain why your choice is correct or better than the others.

   _____

Read Winona's letter to the mayor. Make the needed corrections.

Passage C: Mr. Mayor Letter

1 Dear Mr. Mayor:

2   Last evening my family and I were walking on South Main

3 Street. We noticed litter on the sidewalks and open spaces between

4 the homes. It appeared as if no one had bothered to pick up the

5 paper, bottles or cans in several weeks.

6   As I looked at the trash, I wondered what visitors think. If they

7 are seeing our town for the first time. And finding the large amount of

8 litter. I quickly came to the conclusion that visitors would think no one

9 in the town cared. We both know that is not true. The litter on the

10 sidewalks and in the open lots gives the impression of a town that

11 doesn't care about itself. People should recycle bottles and cans.

12   I would like to propose we start a campaign to get families or

13 groups of people, or clubs to volunteer to clean up sections of our town.

14 We could call the project "Adopt a Street." It would work similar to the

15 "Adopt a Highway Program" run by the government.

16   People would agree to adopt a street, or part of a street, and

17 they would be responsible for cleaning up that area. Prizes for the

18 cleanest areas could be distributed two or three times a year. Plaques

19 could identify who has assumed responsiblity maintaining each area.

20   We need to do something to make this town cleaner. This

21 project would help change the attitude of people toward throwing or

22 dropping containers once they have eaten or used the item inside.

23   My family and I are willing to be the first to volunteer to start the

24   project. We would agree to clean South Main Street from first to third

25   Avenues.

26   Let me know if the Waterville Town Council is in favor of starting this

27   type of project.

28   Yours truly,

29   Winona Tremont

---

1. What change, if any, is needed in lines 3-4 ("We...homes.")?

    A. We noticed litter on the sidewalks. And open spaces between the homes.

    B. We noticed litter on the sidewalks and in the open spaces between the homes.

    C. We noticed litter. On the sidewalks and open spaces between the homes.

    D. Make no change.

2. What is the best way to revise lines 6-8 ("As...litter.")?

    A. As I looked at the trash, I wondered. What would visitors think. If they saw all this trash.

    B. As I looked at the trash. I wondered what visitors seeing our town for the first time. Would think of all the trash.

    C. I looked at the trash and wondered what visitors seeing our town for the first time must think.

    D. Make no change.

3. What would be a good transition word between the sentences in lines 9-11 ("We...itself.")?

    A. And,

    B. While,

    C. Moreover,

    D. Nevertheless,

4. What revision is needed, if any, in lines 12-14 ("I...Street.")?

    A. I would like to propose we start a compaign. To get families, or groups of people, or clubs to volunteer, to clean up sections of our town. We would call the project "Adopt a Street."

    B. I propose we get groups to volunteer to clean up sections of our town. We would call the project "Adopt a Street."

    C. I would like to propose that we start a campaign that would get families, groups of people, or clubs to volunteer to clean up sections of our town. We could call the project "Adopt a Street."

    D. Make no change.

5. What change, if any, is needed in lines 16-17 ("People...area.")?

    A. People would agree to adopt a street, or part of a street and clean it up.

    B. People would agree to clean up an area.

    C. People would agree to adopt a street. Or part of the street. They would be responsible for cleaning that area.

    D. Make no change.

6. What change, if any, is needed in lines 23-25 ("My...Avenues.")?

    A. Change the period after **project** to a comma.

    B. Change **project** to **Project**.

    C. Change **first and third** to **First and Third**.

    D. Make no change.

In the blanks below, write the answer that you chose and the reasons why you think your choice is correct and the others are not.

1. Which answer did you choose? _____
   Briefly explain why your choice is correct or better than the others.

   _____

2. Which answer did you choose? _____
   Briefly explain why your choice is correct or better than the others.

   _____

3. Which answer did you choose? _____
   Briefly explain why your choice is correct or better than the others.

   _____

4. Which answer did you choose? _____
   Briefly explain why your choice is correct or better than the others.

   _____

5. Which answer did you choose? _____
   Briefly explain why your choice is correct or better than the others.

   _____

6. Which answer did you choose? _____
   Briefly explain why your choice is correct or better than the others.

   _____

7. Which answer did you choose? _____
   Briefly explain why your choice is correct or better than the others.

   _____

8. Which answer did you choose? _____
   Briefly explain why your choice is correct or better than the others.

   _____

UNIT 3: Practice Tests

Introduction

The two model tests in this unit include passages representing the types of material you have practiced in the last six chapters. As you take the tests, remember what you have learned in these earlier chapters. These skills will help you know how to read the passages, what the questions are really asking, and how you should answer them. Read each passage carefully, underlining or marking the major points. Then read each multiple-choice question carefully before selecting an answer.

When you have completed this unit, you will have a much better idea of how well you will do on these types of tests. You will also know if there are any areas you will need to review prior to taking an actual writing test.

CHAPTER SEVEN

Practice Test 1

In this chapter, you will be able to practice your skills in revising and editing pieces of writing. There will be a few questions that will ask you to edit punctuation, spelling, and capitalization errors. However, most of the questions will deal with the revising and editing skills that you practiced in Chapters 4 and 5.

Unless you are told that the revising and editing you are being asked to do has some definite skills in mind, you should be prepared to respond to questions that include the whole range of revising and editing skills.

At the end of the chapter, there are several essay topics on which you might be asked to write. To be a successful writer, you need to think of what happens when you look into a mirror. You see your image in reverse. This is very much like the writing process. You write a piece and then see it from a reverse perspective. In the new perspective, you look for flaws or ways to improve the image. Without reflection, you will be incapable of improving your writing.

Passage A: Letter to a Relative

Read the following letter and make the revisions and editing corrections that are necessary.

1 Dear Beth,

2   I know you are not due home from the peace corps for a month. I am

3 writing to invite you to speak to my science class, about the work you have

4 been doing. Bringing electricity to rural towns in which you work. I told the

5 class about what you have been doing since you got there. They are very

6 interested in having you come to talk to them.

7   My science class started to study electricity this week. I told my

8 teacher about how you worked with the villagers where you live to help

9 them, to make their wells run without hand power. Some of the students

10 overheard my conversation with the teacher and they were fascinated by

11 my story. They could not beleive a whole town has no electricity in this day

12 and age. They asked if I would write to you. Inviting you to speak to them,

13 when you are home on vacation. Electricity is very important to people.

14   If you could please bring the diagrams you used to teach the villagers

15 about electricity. Your letters describing what you had to do to help them get

16 over their fear of electricity were fascinating. I was very interested in the two

17 diagrams you included with your last letter. My classmates will be surprised

18 when they see how simple they are. Also, please bring the "before and after"

19 pictures you said you had taken.

20   I hope you will be able to take the time to come to the class. It will be

21 great having my sister as my science teacher. Even if it's only for a day.

22   Love,

    Elaine

1. What change, if any, is needed in the sentence in line 2 ("I...month.")?

    A. Change **know** to **no**.

    B. Change **due** to **dew**.

    C. Change **peace corps** to **Peace Corps**.

    D. Make no change.

2. What transitional word is needed at the beginning of the second sentence ("I...doing.")?

    A. Therefore,

    B. However,

    C. Moreover,

    D. So,

3. What is the best way to combine lines 2-4 ("I...work.")?

    A. I am writing to invite you to speak to my science class about the work you are doing bringing electricity to rural towns.

    B. I am writing to invite you to speak to my science class. About the work you're doing to bring electricity to rural towns.

    C. Please tell my class about electricity in rural towns.

    D. I am writing to you about the work you are doing bringing electricity to rural towns.

4. Where is the best place for the sentence in lines 4-5 ("I...there.")?

    A. after line 4 ("Bringing...work.")

    B. after the sentence in lines 9-11 ("Some...story.")

    C. before line 2

    D. Make no change.

5. What revision, if any, is needed in lines 7-9 ("I...power.")?

    A. I told my teacher about how you worked with the villagers. To make their wells run without hand power.

    B. I told my teacher about the villagers where you live and their wells run by hand power.

    C. I told my teacher about how you worked with the villagers to make their wells run without hand power.

    D. Make no change.

6. What change, if any, is needed in lines 9-11 ("Some...story.")?

    A. Change **students** to **students'**.

    B. Change **overheard** to **overherd**.

    C. Add a comma after **teacher**.

    D. Make no change.

7. What change, if any, is needed in the sentence in lines 11-12 ("They...age.")?

A. Change **beleive** to **believe**.

B. Change **whole** to **hole**.

C. Change **no** to **know**.

D. Make no change.

8. What is the best way to combine the sentences in lines 12-13 ("They...vacation.")?

A. They asked if you would speak to them, if I invited you?

B. They asked if you'd speak to them when you're home on vacation.

C. They asked if I would write to you and invite you to speak to them. When you are home on vacation.

D. They asked me to invite you to speak to them. When you are home on vacation.

9. What change, if any, is needed in lines 14-15 ("If...electricity.")?

A. Put a comma after **could**.

B. Put a comma after **diagrams**.

C. Put a comma after **villagers**.

D. Make no change.

10. Which sentence can be deleted?

A. the sentence in line 2 ("I...month.")

B. the sentence in line 7 ("My...week.")

C. the sentence in lines 13 ("Electricity...people.")

D. the sentence in lines 15-16 ("Your...fascinating.")

Passage B: Letter to Mr. Barlow

Read the following letter and make the revisions and editing corrections that are necessary.

1   Dear Mr. Barlow:

2   I am writing to ask you to change the rule that stops sixth grade

3 students from participating in after-school activities. Last week, I tried out

4 for the basketball team Mr. Schmidt said I was good enough to make the

5 team. But, he said, You can't be on the team because you are only in

6 sixth grade. I feel that is unfair. I am bigger than some seventh graders.

7   When I began talking to other kids in my class, I found that they

8 had the same experience. Many of them had gone to club meetings

9 after school and had been told that they were not able to participate

10 because they were sixth graders.

11   All of us think that excluding sixth graders from after-school activi-

12 ties is unfair. We are members of the Fairway Middle School just like the

13 seventh and eighth graders. All of us can benefit from after-school activi-

14 ties. These clubs give us the chance to explore our interests, learn, and

15 practice our skills and get to meet other students.

16   Also, having our class participate in these activities would allow

17 the school to offer more clubs. Sixth graders should be allowed to join all

18 clubs.

19   I am speaking for many sixth graders. When I ask you to recon-

20 sider the rule that excludes sixth grade students from after-school activi-

21 ties. Please speak with the teachers and see if they would be willing to

22 have this rule changed.

23   Thank you for your consideration of this request.

24   Yours truly,

Jeremy Johnson

1. What change, if any, is needed in lines 3-5 ("Last...team.")?

    A. Last week, I tried out for the basketball team, and Mr. Schmidt said I was good enough to make the team.

    B. Last week, I tried out for the basketball team. And, Mr. Schmidt said I was good enough to make the team.

    C. Last week, I tried out for the basketball team. Mr. Schmidt said, "I was good enough to make the team."

    D. Make no change.

2. What change, if any, is needed in lines 5-6 ("But...grade.")?

    A. But, he said, "You can't be on the team. Because you are only in the sixth grade."

    B. But, he said you can't be on the team because you are in the sixth grade.

    C. But, he said, "You can't be on the team because you are only in the sixth grade."

    D. Make no change.

3. What change, if any, is needed in lines 8-10 ("Many...graders.")?

    A. Many had gone to club meetings after school. And, had been told they weren't able to participate because they were only in sixth grade.

    B. Many had gone to club meetings after school and had been told they were not able to participate. Because they were only in sixth grade.

    C. Many had gone to club meetings. After school, they were told they were not able to participate because they were only in sixth grade.

    D. Make no change.

4. What change, if any, is needed in lines 14-15 ("These...students.")?

    A. These clubs give us the chance to explore our interests.

    B. These clubs give us the chance: to explore our interests, learn and practice our skills, and get to meet other students.

    C. These clubs give us the chance to explore our interests, learn and practice our skills, and meet other students.

    D. Make no change.

5. Which sentence should be deleted from the text?

    A. line 6 ("I...graders.")

    B. lines 12-13 ("We...graders.")

    C. lines 13-14 ("All...activities.")

    D. line 19 ("I...graders.")

6. What would be the best place to move the sentence in lines 17-18 ("Sixth...clubs.")?

    A. in line 6 after "I feel that is unfair."

    B. at the end of paragraph 2, line 10

    C. after the sentence in lines 13-14, "All...activities."

    D. at the end of paragraph 5, line 22

7. What change, if any, is needed in lines 19-21 ("I...activities.")?

    A. I am speaking for many sixth graders when I ask you to reconsider the rule. That excludes sixth graders from after-school activities.

    B. I am speaking for many sixth graders when I ask you to reconsider the rule that excludes sixth graders from after-school activities.

    C. I am speaking. For many sixth grade students. When I ask you to reconsider the rule excluding sixth graders from after-school activities.

    D. Make no change.

Passage C: Letter to Advice Columnist

Read the following letter and make the revisions and editing corrections that are necessary.

1   Dear Advice Columnist:

2   My parents will not give me permission to attend the Harrison

3   Middle School Activity Night. How can I get them to change their minds.

4   Activity Night is filled with lots of fun things to do.

5   My problems started right after my last report card. I admit my

6   grades had slipped from the first marking period when my parents saw

7   my latest report card, they got upset. They made me give up all evening

8   activities until my marks improved.

9   It has been six weeks since I was grounded, and my marks have

10   been improving. Each teacher I have says I am doing much better than

11   last marking period. The problem is my father will not lift the ban on

12   evening activities. Until he sees my next report card. By then, it will be

13   too late! The report cards come out two days after Activity Night.

14   I guess I can't really blame my dad for not believing me about my

15   grades. Before this last report card he said he thought that I was out so

16   much he was concerned about my grades. I told him not to worry.

17   Everything was under control. Unfortunately, it wasn't, and I received

18   two failures on my report card. Now, when I say things are getting

19   better, his response is let's wait until we see your report card.

20   Can you suggest how I can show him that I am really telling the

21   truth? I am doing better!

22   Please hurry,

   Sheila

1. What punctuation, if any, is needed in line 3 ("How...minds.")?

    A. Add a comma after **How**.

    B. Add a comma after **them**.

    C. Change the period to a question mark.

    D. Make no change.

2. What change, if any, is needed in lines 5-7 ("I...upset.")?

    A. I admit my marks had slipped and when my parents saw my report card they were upset.

    B. I admit my marks had slipped from my first report card. When my parents saw my latest report, they got upset.

    C. I admit my marks slipped from my first report card. When my parents, saw my latest report card, they got upset.

    D. Make no change.

3. What change, if any, is needed in lines 9-10 ("It...improving.")?

    A. It has been six weeks. Since I was grounded. My marks have been improving.

    B. It has been six weeks, since I was grounded and my marks have been improving.

    C. It has been six weeks. Since I was grounded, and my marks have been improving.

    D. Make no change.

4. What change, if any, is needed in lines 10-11 ("Each...period.")?

    A. Each teacher that I have, says I am doing much better, than last marking period.

    B. Each teacher I have, says that I am doing much better than last year.

    C. Each teacher I have says, "I have been doing better than the last marking period."

    D. Make no change.

5. What change, if any, is needed in lines 11-12 ("The...card.")?

    A. The problem is that my father will not lift the ban on evening activities until he sees my next report card.

    B. The problem is my father. My ban on evening activities will not be lifted. Until my next report card.

    C. The problem is my father will not lift the ban on evening activities; until he sees my next report card.

    D. Make no change.

6. What change, if any, is needed in lines 15-16 ("Before...grades.")?

    A. Before this report card, he said I was out too much. He was concerned about my grades.

    B. Before this report card, he said I was out too much. And he was concerned about my grades.

    C. Before this last report card, he said he thought I was out so much. He was concerned about my grades.

    D. Make no change.

7. What change, if any, is needed in lines 18-19 ("Now...card.")?

    A. Now, when I say things are getting better, his response is let's wait and see your report card.

    B. Now, when I say things are getting better, he responds, "Let's wait and see your report card."

    C. Now when I say things are getting better, he responds let's wait and see your report card.

    D. Make no change.

8. Which sentence can be deleted?

    A. the sentence in line 4 ("Activity...do.")

    B. the sentence in lines 12-13 ("By...late!")

    C. the sentence in lines 14-15 ("I...grades.")

    D. the sentence in line 17 ("Everything...control.")

Passage D: Mountains

Read the following report and make the revisions and editing corrections that are necessary.

1   One thing that has always interested me is mountains. There are

2   not any very high mountains in our part of the state. When my family

3   traveled to Montana and Colorado last summer, we saw some very large

4   mountains. It was cold up there and there was snow. This fascinated

5   me, and I thought it would be interesting to learn more about some of the

6   highest mountains in the world.

7   I decided to concentrate my research on the highest mountains on

8   each of the continents. What I discovered is, that what many people

9   refer to as mountains are insignificant in comparison to the really tall

10   mountains of the world. The term "mountain" isn't determined by the

11   actual size of the mountains.

12   The tallest mountain in Antarctica is a mountain named Vinson

13   Massif. It is in the Ellsworth mountains in Western Antarctica. This moun-

14   tain is 16,864 feet high. Although it is the tallest mountain on this conti-

15   nent, it is the smallest in comparison to the highest mountains on the

16   other continents. Asia has the highest mountain.

17   Europe's highest mountain is in what was part of the Union of

18   Soviet Socialist Republics (U.S.S.R.). But, Mount Elbrus is in the Caucasus

19   mountains in the Kabardin-Balkar Republic. It is 18,481 feet high. People

20   might expect the highest mountain to be in the Alps.

21   On the continent of Africa, the Kibo peak of Kilimanjaro is the

22   highest point. It is 19,340 feet high. The mountain is near the border of

23   the country of Kenya. It seems strange to think of snowcapped moun-

24   tains near the Equator, but they are because of their altitude.

25   Mount Aconcague is South America's highest peak. It is in the

26   Andes Mountains in Argentina, not far from the border with Chile. This

27   mountain is 22,835 feet high. It is not only the highest mountain in South

28   America. It is also the highest mountain in the Western Hemisphere.

29   It probably doesn't surprise anyone that the highest mountain in

30   North America is in Alaska. Mount McKinley in Denali National Park is

31   the highest peak. It is 20,320 feet high. This mountain in central Alaska is

32   also known as Denali. However, it is not the highest mountain in this

33   hemisphere.

34   The highest mountain in the world, of course, is Mount Everest at

35   29,028 feet. It is in the Himalayas in Asia. The mountain is located on the

36   border of Nepal and Tibet. This is probably the best known mountain of

37   the group of mountains.

38   Three of the highest mountains are probably quite familiar names

39   to people, but two are relatively unknown to the general public. Others

40   must share curiosity about mountains, too. So many people seem to feel

41   the need to climb these giants.

1. What is a good transitional word to use before the sentence in lines 2-4 ("When...mountains.")?

    A. So,

    B. Besides,

    C. However,

    D. As a result,

2. What change, if any, is needed in line 4 ("It...snow.")?

    A. It was cold up there; and there was snow.

    B. It was cold and snowy up there.

    C. It was cold up there. And it snowed.

    D. Make no change.

3. What change, if any, is needed in lines 4-6 ("This...world.")?

    A. This fascinated me. And, I thought it would be interesting to learn more about some of the highest mountains in the world.

    B. This fascinated me, I thought. It would be interesting to learn more about some of the highest mountains in the world.

    C. This fascinated me and I thought. It would be interesting to learn more about some of the highest mountains in the world.

    D. Make no change.

4. What change, if any, is needed in lines 8-10 ("What...world.")?

    A. What I discovered is that what many people refer to as mountains are insignificant in comparison to the really tall mountains of the world.

    B. What I discovered is that what many people refer to as mountains are insignificant. When compared to the tallest mountains.

    C. What I discovered is that what many people refer to as mountains, are insignificant. In comparison to the really tall mountains of the world.

    D. Make no change.

5. What sentence, if any, should be deleted?

    A. the sentence in lines 1-2 ("There...state.")

    B. the sentence in lines 10-11 ("The...mountains.")

    C. the sentence in line 16 ("Asia...mountain.")

    D. Make no change.

6. Where is the best place to move paragraph 7 ("It...hemisphere.")?

    A. after paragraph 1

    B. after paragraph 2

    C. after paragraph 3

    D. after paragraph 4

7. What is the best way to revise paragraph 4 ("Europe's...Alps.")?

    A. Move the last sentence in the paragraph before the first sentence in the paragraph.

    B. Move the last sentence in the paragraph after the first sentence in the paragraph.

    C. Move the last sentence in the paragraph after the second sentence in the paragraph.

    D. Make no change.

8. Where is the best place to move the sentence in lines 38-39 ("Three...public.")?

    A. at the end of paragraph 1

    B. at the end of paragraph 2

    C. at the end of paragraph 3

    D. at the end of paragraph 4

WRITING TASKS

Write an essay about one or more of these topics. Follow your teacher's instructions. Remember to edit and revise your work and to use a pre-writing strategy to help you organize your ideas.

1. Write a letter to someone who you would like to come to speak to students in one of your classes. Choose a person who you would like to meet and with whom you and your classmates might like to spend some time discussing topics of mutual interest.

2. Write a letter to your school newspaper expressing your views on some school subject. It may be something that you favor or something to which you are opposed.

CHAPTER EIGHT

Practice Test 2

In this chapter you will have the opportunity to practice some of the writing skills that you might expect to find on standardized or state writing tests. There are writing prompts as well as selections that you will have to revise and edit.

How well you do on the materials in this chapter will give you some idea of how you might do on large-scale writing tests. You will be able to have a better idea of any skills that you will need to spend more time learning and which ones you know quite well.

Remember to use all of the strategies you have learned about the writing process.

Passage A: Letter to Sally

Read the following letter and make the revisions and editing corrections that are necessary.

1 Dear Sally,

2   I really enjoyed the surprise birthday party you gave for me on

3 Saturday. When you invited me to your house for the night, I never dreamed

4 it was just to celebrate my birthday. Surprise parties usually aren't surprises

5 for the person involved they only act surprised to please their friends and

6 family. What had me completely fooled was that my birthday wasn't until

7 the following Thursday.

8   When I walked in your front door I was sure that only your family was

9 at home. In fact, I thought I might have come on the wrong night. For the

10 sleep over. Because the living room was dark. When I walked in and every-

11 one sang "Happy birthday," I nearly collapsed from shock. It was a total sur-

12 prise.

13   You know how much I like ice cream and having a birthday ice

14 cream cake was perfect. The cake was delicious. I could have eaten two

15 more slices without any trouble. The cookies you and our friends baked were

16 very good, too. It was a great party.

17   Thank you for all chipping in to buy me the CD player. I have been

18 asking my parents for one for the last month. I was hoping they would buy

19 one for me for my birthday. You all knew exactly what I wanted. Now, I can

20 ask my folks for some CDs to play on it.

21   I am lucky to have such good friends as you. Thanks again for a very

22 special party.

23   Your friend,

24   Ginger

1. What change, if any, is needed in lines 2-3 ("I...Saturday.")?

    A. Change **really** to **real**.

    B. Change **surprise** to **surprize**.

    C. Change **birthday party** to **Birthday Party**.

    D. Make no change.

2. What change, if any, is needed in lines 4-6 ("Surprise...family.")?

    A. Change **surprise** and **surprises** to **surprize** and **surprizes**.

    B. Change **usually** to **usualy**.

    C Add a semicolon after **involved**.

    D. Make no change.

3. What revision, if any, is needed in lines 9-10 ("In...dark.")?

    A. In fact, I thought I might have come on the wrong night for the sleepover. Because the living room was dark.

    B. In fact, I thought I might have come on the wrong night. For the sleepover, because the living room was dark.

    C. In fact, I thought I might have come on the wrong night for the sleepover because the living room was dark.

    D. Make no change.

4. Which sentence should be deleted from the text, if any?

    A. lines 4-6 ("Suprise...family.")

    B. lines 6-7 ("What...Thursday.")

    C. lines 14-15 ("I...trouble.")

    D. Make no change.

5. What change, if any, is needed in lines 10-11 ("When...shock.")?

    A. Add a comma after **in**.

    B. Change **birthday** to **Birthday**.

    C. Change the comma after the word **birthday** to a period.

    D. Make no change.

6. Where, if any place, should the sentence in line 19 be moved ("You...wanted.")?

    A. before line 17 ("Thank...player.")

    B. after line 17 ("Thank...player.")

    C. after lines 19-20 ("Now...it.")

    D. Make no change.

Passage B: Letter to Dr. Johnson

Read the following letter and make the revisions and editing corrections that are necessary.

1   Dr. Walter Johnson, Superintendent

2   Midvalley School District

3   Midvalley, PA 17888

4   Dear Dr. Johnson:

5   Recently our school policy on making up class assignments when a

6   student is absent from school has been changed. Now anyone who is absent

7   must make up all class work. Within two days of the date when the absence

8   occurred. Other schools don't have this policy.

9   I think this policy change is very unfair. Two days does not give stu-

10 dents a chance to complete these assignments adequately. The first day

11 after an absence is spent catching up in class and finding out the next day's

12 assignments. That night must be devoted to both getting ready for the next

13 day and completing this missed work. This new policy requires students to

14 prepare for two days of assignments in one evening.

15   When you consider that a student who is absent misses up to seven

16 classes a day, the situation becomes impossible. Before, each teacher would

17 decide how long students could take to complete missed assignments. Last

18 time I was absent for two days, it took me two days to catch up in class and

19 five days to complete the assignments I had missed in my seven classes. It

20 would have been impossible for me to get these assignments done within two

21 days. Let alone prepare for my next day classes.

22   I do not understand the reason for changing the policy. We go to

23 school to learn. Under this new policy, the goal seems to be to complete

24 assignments just to meet a policy deadline creates poor learning.

25   I urge the Administration to rethink its new policy. On making up

26   class assignments. The amount of time to be given to doing this should be left

27   to the teachers in each class to decide. They know the amount of time it may

28   take to complete their assignments.

29   Thank you for considering my request.

30   Sincerely,

          Seth Sewell

---

1. What change, if any, is needed in lines 5-6 ("Recently...changed.")?

   A. Add a comma after **Recently**.

   B. Change **school policy** to **School Policy**.

   C. Add a comma after **assignments** and a comma after **absent**.

   D. Make no change.

2. What revision, if any, is needed in lines 6-8 ("Now...occurred.")?

   A. Now, anyone who is absent from school. Must make up all class work within two days.

   B. Now, anyone who is absent from school must make up all class work within two days of the date when the absence occurred.

   C. Now, anyone absent from school must make up school work. Within two days of when the absence occurred.

   D. Make no change.

3. What change, if any, is needed in lines 10-12 ("The...assignments.")?

   A. The first day, after the absence, is spent catching up in class and finding out the next day's assignments.

   B. The first day, after the absence, is spent catching up in class, and finding out the next day's assignments.

   C. The first day after the absence, is spent catching up in class and finding out the next day's assignments.

   D. Make no change.

4. Where is the best place for the sentence in lines 16-17 ("Before...assignments.")?

   A. after lines 6-7 ("Now...work.")

   B. after lines 7-8 ("Within...occurred.")

   C. after lines 13-14 ("This...evening.")

   D. after lines 21 ("Let...classes.")

5. What revision, if any, is needed in lines 17-19 ("Last...classes.")?

    A. Last time, I was absent for two days. It took me two days to catch up in class. And five days to complete the assignments I had missed in my seven classes.

    B. Last time I was absent for two days it took me two days to catch up in class. And five days to complete assignments I had missed in my seven classes.

    C. Last time I was absent for two days it took me two days to catch up in class and five days to complete assignments in my seven classes.

    D. Make no change.

6. What change, if any, is needed in lines 19-21 ("It...classes.")

    A. It would have been impossible for me to get these assignments done within two days, let alone prepare for my next day classes.

    B. It would have been impossible, for me to get these assignments done, within two days. Let alone prepare for my next day classes.

    C. It would have been impossible for me to get these assignments done within two days. Let alone prepare for my next day classes.

    D Make no change.

7. What change, if any, is needed in lines 23-24 ("Under...learning.")?

    A. Under the new policy the goal seems to be to complete assignments, learning is secondary.

    B. Under this new policy, the goal seems to be to complete assignments; learning is secondary.

    C. Under this new policy, the goal seems to be to complete assignments, learning is secondary.

    D. Make no change.

8. What change, if any, is needed in lines 25-26 ("I...assignments.")?

    A. Change **Administration** to **administration**.

    B. Change **its** to **it's**.

    C. Add a comma after **Administration**.

    D. Make no change.

Passage C: Letter to Advice Columnist

Read the following letter and make the revisions and editing corrections that are necessary.

1   Dear Frannie:

2   I need help! My step-brother is picking on me. During the past month.

3   It has gotten so bad, I don't even want to be in the same room with him.

4   When my mother first married his father, B.J. and me we got along

5   fine. We went everywhere together. Last spring he even joined my baseball

6   team, and he helped us get into a championship game. We lost but every-

7   one said we played an outstanding game.

8   Beginning in September, things started to change. When we would

9   be wrestling for fun, he seemed to be trying to hurt me. Other times, he

10   would be his old self and we would have fun. Sometimes I think our troubles

11   could have something to do with school. B.J. is not as good a student as I

12   am. However I can't be sure it's school because there are times he picks on

13   me when there haven't been any phone calls from the school about B.J.

14   Recently, he started asking me for money. He seems to be broke all

15   the time. When I say I don't have any money, he gets mad. One time I

16   caught him going through things in my room. When I walked in the door, he

17   looked at me and said I thought I left something in here. He never did say

18   what it was.

19   Now, he makes fun of me because my voice is changing. Sometimes

20   it cracks and sounds funny when I talk. He even criticizes the way I dress.

21   Nothing I do seems to be all right in his eyes.

22   I haven't told my mom or my step-dad about any of this. I don't want

23   to cause any trouble between them. I don't want my mom to worry about

24   me. Also, I was afraid my step-dad would think I was being a baby. He

25   might side with B.J., and he and I were just beginning to get along pretty

26   well.

27 Do you have any suggestions about how I can get my step-brother to

28 quit picking on me. I really would like us all to get along and be a real

29 family.

30 Confused,

31 Mitch

---

1. What revision, if any, is needed in lines 2-3 ("During...him.")?

   A. During the past month. It has gotten so bad. I don't even want to be in the same room with him.

   B. During the past month, it has gotten so bad. I don't even want to be in the same room with him.

   C. During the past month, it has gotten so bad that I don't even want to be in the same room with him.

   D. Make no change.

2. What change, if any, is needed in lines 4-5 ("When...fine.")?

   A. Change **mother** and **father** to **Mother** and **Father**.

   B. Change **me** and **we** to **I** and delete **we**.

   C. Change **along** to **a long**.

   D Make no change.

3. What change is needed in lines 5-7 ("Last...game.")?

   A. Change **baseball team** to **Baseball Team**.

   B. Change **spring** to **Spring**.

   C. Add a comma after **spring**.

   D. Delete the comma after **team**.

4. What change, if any, is needed in lines 9-10 ("Other...fun.")?

   A. Delete the comma after **times**.

   B. Add a comma after **self**.

   C. Change the period to an exclamation point.

   D. Make no change.

5. What change, if any, is needed in lines 12-13 ("However...B.J.")?

    A. Add a comma after **However**.

    B. Change **it's** to **its**.

    C. Change **can't** to **cant**.

    D. Make no change.

6. What change, if any, is needed in lines 16-17 ("When...here.")?

    A. When I walked in the door. He looked at me and said, "I thought I left something in here."

    B. When I walked in the door, he looked at me and said, I thought I left something in here.

    C. When I walked in the door, he looked at me and said, "I thought I left something in here."

    D. Make no change.

7. Which sentence, if any, should be deleted?

    A. lines 6-7 ("We...game.")

    B. line 11 ("B.J...am.")

    C. lines 17-18 ("He...was.")

    D. line 21 ("Nothing...eyes.")

8. What change, if any, is needed in lines 24-26 ("He...well.")?

    A. Delete the comma after **B.J.**

    B. Change **he and I** to **him and me**.

    C. Change **well** to **good**.

    D. Make no change.

9. What change, if any, is needed in lines 27-28 ("Do...me.")?

    A. Add a period after **suggestions** and begin **about** with a capital letter.

    B. Add a comma after **about**.

    C. Change the period after **me** to a question mark.

    D. Make no change.

10. What change, if any, is needed in lines 28-29 ("I...family.")?

    A. Change **along** to **a long**.

    B. Add a comma after **along**.

    C. Add a period after **along** and begin **and** with a capital.

    D. Make no change.

Passage D: What Price Tennis?

Read the following report and make the revisions and editing corrections that are necessary.

1   Marianna is an outstanding athlete. She is very good in basketball

2   and in softball. She is especially good at tennis. Her parents think she may

3   be good enough to become a professional tennis player. Marianna is thir-

4   teen.

5   Her parents spoke to several tennis coaches about their daughters

6   ability. All of them encouraged the family. To find an outstanding coach.

7   With experience in training professional tennis players to coach Marianna.

8   There are many excellent coaches in Florida. Unfortunately, that would

9   mean either Marianna would have to leave home or the family would have

10   to relocate.

11   Mr. and Mrs. Walker discussed their options. Mr. Walker said that he

12   could ask his company for a transfer to one of their other locations. He isn't

13   sure the company will or can arrange this. And he is uncertain what effect a

14   transfer will have on his job or on his salary.

15   Mrs. Walker believes she can find a new position. She knows that

16   nurses are in demand. Her experience in the hospital emergency room

17   makes her very confident. That she will have little trouble finding a new job.

18   What Mr. and Mrs. Walker didn't count on is the opposition from their

19   children about moving. Rashaun is interested in supporting Marianna's

20   tennis career, but he feels he will have difficulty getting a college scholarship

21   in a new school. He is a candidate for a scholar-athlete scholarship in his

22   high school. Rashaun doesn't plan on a professional career in athletics, but

23   he is good enough to attract the attention of scouts from some good colleges.

24   He wants to major in engineering. A scholarship will be helpful in paying his

25   college expenses.

26   Didi also has reservations about moving. She is interested in a career

27   in international banking or marketing. Her excellent grades in foreign lan-

28   guages and economics might be difficult to maintain in a new school.

29   Even Marianna has some concerns about their possible relocation

30   plans. She wonders if she's really good enough to be a tennis pro. She appre-

31   ciates the sacrifices her parents are prepared to make to help her. She under-

32   stands her brother's and sister's apprehension about changing schools. They

33   aren't being selfish, their futures can be greatly affected by this decision.

34   The Walker family is faced with a major decision. They propose hold-

35   ing a family conference to discuss the situation. Each person will be free to

36   express opinions on the subject of moving to Florida. They will then take a

37   vote. They all agree they will abide by what the majority think is in the best

38   interests of the family.

---

1. What is the best transition word to insert
   before for the sentence in line 2
   ("She...tennis.")?

   A. Therefore,

   B. Since,

   C. However,

   D. Nevertheless,

2. What change, if any, is needed in lines 5-6
   ("Her...ability.")?

   A. Change **spoke** to **spoken**.

   B. Change **their** to **there**.

   C. Change **daughters** to **daughter's**.

   D. Make no change.

3. What is the best way to revise lines 6-7 ("All...Marianna.")?

    A. All of them encouraged the family to find an outstanding professional tennis coach for Marianna.

    B. All of them have encouraged the family to find an outstanding coach. With experience in training professional players. To coach Marianna.

    C. All of them encouraged the family to get professional coaching.

    D. All of them encouraged getting an outstanding coach of professional tennis players.

4. What change, if any, is needed in lines 11-14 ("Mr. Walker...salary.")?

    A. Mr. Walker said, "That he could ask his company for a transfer." He isn't sure they will do it. And he is uncertain what his job or salary will be.

    B. Mr. Walker said he could ask his company for a transfer, but he isn't sure he will get it. Moreover, he doesn't know what effect a transfer might have on his job or his salary.

    C. Mr. Walker is going to ask for a transfer to a new location. He said, "The company might not want to do this." In addition, he doesn't know what his job or salary will be.

    D. Mr. Walker thinks his company will give him a transfer if he asks for it. However, he is uncertain what effect the transfer will have on his job or his salary.

5. What is the best transition word to insert before for the sentence in lines 15-16?

    A. Therefore,

    B. Moreover,

    C. However,

    D. Since,

6. What change, if any, is needed in lines 16-17 ("Her...job.")?

    A. Delete the period and change **That** to **that**.

    B. Change the period to a comma and change **That** to **that**.

    C. Change the period to a semicolon and change **That** to **that**.

    D. Make no change.

7. What change, if any, is needed in lines 22-23 ("Rashaun...colleges.")?

    A. Change **professional** to **Professional**.

    B. Change **scouts** to **Scouts**.

    C. Change **colleges** to **Colleges**.

    D. Make no change.

8. What change, if any, is needed in lines 32-33 ("They...decision.")?

    A. Change **greatly** to **great**.

    B. Change **affected** to **effected**.

    C. Change the comma to a semicolon.

    D. Make no change.

WRITING TASKS

Write an essay about one or more of these topics. Follow your teacher's instructions. Remember to edit and revise your work and to use a pre-writing strategy to help you organize your ideas.

1. In many parts of the world, people are eager to have the privilege of being able to vote for those who will run their government. However, in the United States, where we have this privilege, only about half of those who are eligible to vote do vote, even in our major elections.

   Write an essay telling why you think so many of our citizens don't vote, what effect this may have on our government, and what you think could be done to get more people to vote.

2. Imagine that you had the opportunity to join a team of mountain climbers that was going to climb one of the highest mountain peaks. Tell how you would feel about this invitation and describe your reasons for either accepting or declining the invitation.

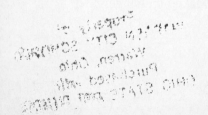